CW00551525

STRETCHING THE BOUNDARIES – SIDEWAYS

The Story of a Side-Saddle Champion

Rayna Matthews

ARTHUR H. STOCKWELL LTD
Torrs Park, Ilfracombe, Devon, EX34 8BA
Established 1898
www.ahstockwell.co.uk

© *Rayna Matthews, 2018*
First published in Great Britain, 2018
All rights reserved.
No part of this publication may be reproduced
or transmitted in any form or by any means,
electronic or mechanical, including photocopy,
recording, or any information storage and
retrieval system, without permission
in writing from the copyright holder.

British Library Cataloguing-in-Publication Data.
A catalogue record for this book is available
from the British Library.

ISBN 978-0-7223-4833-8
Printed in Great Britain by
Arthur H. Stockwell Ltd
Torrs Park   Ilfracombe
Devon EX34 8BA

DEDICATION

To my dear husband, Bill.
He kept on seeing ways around problems
to make sure that I didn't give up.

ACKNOWLEDGEMENTS

This book would never have become a reality without the help
and advice of these friends –

Ben Read, for his many hours spent typing and correcting my
script.
Julian Hibbert, for his assistance with my manuscript.
And the many other friends who helped and encouraged me.

FOREWORD BY JANE

Rayna Matthews has presented a fast-moving and inspirational story of her life's work helping others afflicted by disability.

Severely disabled herself since the age of thirty-three from an attack of polio, she refused to give in and take no for an answer; instead, through her love of horses and knowledge of the benefits of riding as a therapy, she set herself challenges few would ever have contemplated. She proved she could overcome most of her problems through sheer guts and determination, with great support from her friends, her long-suffering husband and some special horses over the years. It was often a matter of "If at first you don't succeed, try, try and try again" and certainly Rayna met more than her fair share of ups and downs, facing many rebuffs and often having to jump through hoops and climb mountains to succeed.

In this book she propels the reader through numerous situations both encouraging and depressing in their outcomes. Throughout it all, however, her upbeat attitude shows so clearly how being positive can often overcome huge obstacles.

Rayna's infectious can-do attitude and successes with her riding soon led to other riders wanting to join her. It was not too long before she had encouraged so many others in situations similar to hers to follow her example and ride within the Riding for the Disabled Association or side-saddle groups. She set up TRADISTAR and gave side-saddle displays both at home and abroad, often in beautifully home-made costumes.

Always supremely elegant, my abiding memory of Rayna Matthews is giving a stunning display of side-saddle riding at the RDA National Championships which inspired all who saw it – a career highlight and an illustration of her quest to help others make their lives better, despite their challenges. A truly remarkable story of a very dedicated, determined, talented and inspirational woman.

Jane Holderness-Roddam CBE, LVO

CHAPTER ONE

Early Days

This is the story of a twenty-year journey that began as a result of becoming disabled. It's about a world of equestrian enthusiasm and the horses that played a major part in my life.

I'm now closer to eighty than seventy years old and a long way from where I began in Sydney, Australia. From a very young age it was apparent that I had a passion for horses, and this has strengthened over my lifetime.

Luckily, my parents realised my growing devotion and rather cautiously let me have my first pony when I was ten years old. From then on, and throughout my teens, riding and competing on horseback became an important part of my life. Often, I had to make deals with my parents that I would do my homework, music practice, and other sports before the equine activities.

During these years I was a keen pony-club member and a successful competitor in showing and dressage. I had a number of years' success with a 14.2-hand palomino pony called Dawn. She was followed by a much-envied Arab called Zilfred.

The Sydney riding club that I belonged to invited well-known equestrian personalities to Australia to judge and give training clinics. Still in my teens, I can remember being invited to be a guinea pig for Captain Kussakoff and Colonel Llewellyn during their visit. Another interesting guest was the

American actor who played Hopalong Cassidy. My riding club worked very hard to perfect a 'square dancing on horseback' routine, which made a spectacular display for his visit.

While still in my teens I dreamed of becoming a vet. Then, on holiday one summer at my grandparents' farm, I witnessed a vet artificially inseminating a cow; this certainly put the kibosh on that plan! The female vet put on some overalls, lifted up the startled animal's tail with her right hand, then plunged her left arm into the poor creature's back end. She was up to her armpit in muck – no gloves, no protection! I was shocked and disgusted. If that's what vetting is all about, I felt, it's not for me!

Upon leaving school I was undecided about what to do with my life. My mother suggested a year at finishing school, which I enjoyed. I also learnt some skills at millinery.

It had soon dawned on me that a nursing career might be an alternative to animal husbandry, so by my nineteenth birthday I was in uniform and had started work in a children's ward at a large district hospital.

By my early twenties, my work and intentions to travel meant that I had to part company with equestrian activities.

With a pretty solid nursing career under my belt I set off for London, as many young Australians did in the 1960s and '70s. This was not only to further their professions and studies, but also to see something of the big, wide world.

One evening, when I was living in London, I was on my way home from my job as a private 'special' nurse. It had been snowing, and there was a foot of deep melting snow and slush on the ground. As I was crossing the street on a zebra crossing in Kensington I was knocked down by a young driver of an MG sports car, carried, so I'm told, some distance down the street, and pinned between a building and the front of his car. There were multiple fractures and other injuries, followed by thirteen months in hospital and a rehabilitation centre. It was recorded, for insurance purposes, that I had suffered forty per cent disability from my injuries.

Returning to Australia, the next ten years were spent putting a new career together and generally trying to make a full recovery. As part of my work with the Maternal and Child Health Bureau, some of the nurses and doctors, including me, as I was to travel to other countries as part of my job, were given the polio vaccine because of their work with children.

One day, not long after this, I went to work as usual. As the day wore on I became very ill, with flu-like symptoms and an uncontrollable cough. On my way home I decided that a visit to my GP was necessary. He was somewhat alarmed by my dramatic symptoms; however, I managed to get myself home and put myself to bed after taking the medication which he had prescribed. By the next morning I was unable to lift my head from the pillow and it had become worryingly difficult to breathe. I felt that I would die! I was referred to a leading physician at a top Sydney teaching hospital. This doctor was even more baffled by my strange paralytic symptoms and referred me to the psychiatric unit at the same hospital. These were the days when often if a patient was presented with strange or unrecognised symptoms it was thought that it could be a problem 'in your head'. However, a diagnosis was not offered.

I was adamant that this was not for me and returned home. It took over a year to recover from this episode and about eighteen months before I managed to get back to full-time work.

My job in healthcare was developing rather rapidly into a specialisation with children with hearing problems, particularly in infants and babies. By this time I had accrued some study leave and it was recommended that I go to a specialised hospital in England to further my studies in this field.

When I reached London I was still struggling with physical tiredness and often needed to spend much of my weekend in bed in order to get through the week at work.

One day, while shopping on the King's Road in Chelsea, I collapsed and found myself completely unable to walk. Once again I returned to hospital, where the physicians and neurologists put me through a battery of tests, all of which came back as normal. Though baffled, their only recommendation was for me to be seen by the 'head shrink'. Of course, I didn't have any condition that made me need this kind of help.

Several months went by and I managed to get a job in the NHS that would fit my stamina, or lack of it.

Meanwhile, during my efforts to return to full-time work, I met a charming English gentleman by the name of Bill. He had invited me out a couple of times and I was beginning to enjoy his attentions. One morning I left my home for my office in Westminster Hospital, a journey that usually took fifteen to twenty minutes. One hour later I collapsed on the hospital doorstep.

This time I was rushed to the Royal Free, an isolation hospital in Hampstead. As the ambulance drove through London with its siren wailing, I can remember thinking that I'd seen the last of that nice man I'd just met. How wrong was I! That evening he made his way to the hospital and tracked me down. From that evening onwards I cherished his company and regular visits.

This hospital was very sympathetic to my condition and thought that they understood my symptoms. They likened them to an epidemic that had broken out at the hospital sometime previously, and the patients' symptoms were similar to mine but not so severe. Eventually I was given a label for my condition – myalgic encephalomyelitis, otherwise known as chronic fatigue syndrome, an illness which is characterised by extreme weakness and tiredness. However, my condition seemed more paralytic, with an inability to walk without the aid of two sticks and a wheelchair requirement for any distance travel.

From the Royal Free I was transferred back to the Westminster Hospital, where I could recover among friends and colleagues.

One day Bill asked the sister on the ward if he could take me for a little outing. "Only two hours," she said sternly, and so, still in my dressing gown, he helped me into his classic Princess car and drove me to a beautiful antique jewellery shop in Church Street, Kensington. He sat me down at a viewing table and my eyes stood out of my head on stalks at what was placed in front of me: dazzlingly beautiful rings, brooches, necklaces and other wonderful jewellery. We were served tea in antique cups and saucers and I was made to feel very special.

"Choose one to wear now, for our engagement, and a second one for our wedding!" said Bill.

None of this had been mentioned to me before, but, as it was suggested that I should go home to Australia to be cared for by my mother, this was becoming exciting news. When we returned to my hospital bed the reaction of the nurses was spectacular.

We were married in Sydney and brave Bill became both husband and carer. After a short honeymoon we returned to London, but it became evident that my job was too taxing on my health. I therefore had no choice but to retire.

CHAPTER TWO

I Meet Waltzie

Aware of my love of horses, one day Bill took me to the Horse of the Year Show at Wembley. There we passed a booth that was set up by the Riding for the Disabled Association (RDA). We were both quite taken aback by this and struck up a conversation with the RDA representatives. Our hopes weren't very high as I was in my wheelchair and couldn't imagine that horse riding would be even remotely possible. There we met a lady by the name of Sue Adams and Bill mentioned to her that I had been a keen rider in the past and dreamed of doing it again, if at all possible.

"That's what we're here for," said Sue. "That's what we do." She then went on to suggest we contact the London group that operated at Wormwood Scrubs.

This facility was run by Sister Mary Joy, a nun from the Order of the Baby Jesus and a dear soul. She had a very impressive RDA set up – she owned several lovely ponies, had helpers and instructors, and an indoor school which had recently been opened by Princess Anne, who is, by the way, the patron of the RDA.

After a year or more of my badgering, Sister Mary Joy took pity on me and agreed to take me on.

I started attending the centre once a week for half an hour. This was in 1994. On our first visit we were given a guided tour by a lovely young lady called Jane. I fell in love with a little chestnut gelding called Quizzy, and met Topaz the goat as well as three dogs and three cats. The next time I visited I rode in a group of disabled riders, on none other than my beloved Quizzy!

Johan was our young teacher and, because of my previous experience with my own ponies and horses, it wasn't long before I was allowed to ride unaided.

Coming back to riding after thirty years, although this time as a disabled rider, was the beginning of a new and wonderful life, one which was very unselfishly encouraged by my husband.

It didn't take me long to get into my stride again, but there was one terrible problem: as we progressed into an active trot my legs would go into painful spasms. This began to unbalance me, and I started to have doubts whether I would be able to develop the canter. Hope was not lost, however, and in May Sister Mary Joy entered me into the centre's dressage competition on Quizzy. To my considerable surprise I won the class! During the competition I was observed by a captain who trained the Household Cavalry, and he suggested that I take up dressage as a sport. I was also fortunate to be allowed to ride Sister Mary Joy's horse, on which she competed in dressage.

At this time I had a part-time lecturing job at Westminster College in fashion, design and tailoring. One lunchtime I happened to sit next to the college administrator, Neal Friar. Rather than talk shop, I told him that I was currently riding with a group of disabled riders. I must have struck a chord with him because he told me that his mother was seventy-six years old and rode and hunted side-saddle. My jaw dropped! As far as I knew only the Queen rode side-saddle, but my curiosity had been aroused.

"I must meet your Mum" was my response.

It was a two-and-a-half-hour drive from London to

Billingshurst on the next day to meet Cecily Friar. I was met with a warm welcome – something I would grow accustomed to on many more occasions when meeting other side-saddle riders. Cecily, now the late Cecily Friar, was a founding member of the present-day Side Saddle Association (SSA). Her daughter Vanessa still runs their farm and keeps all the horses.

Cecily had a dear old 'schoolmistress' called Waltzie, on which I could get started riding side-saddle. Waltzie was saddled up and I was helped to 'get on board'. Getting from a wheelchair on to a 16.2-hand horse with a side-saddle that stood another five or six inches on top of that is not the easiest of procedures! However, Waltzie was a kind old mare and after about ten minutes I was beginning to like this way of riding. I felt safe and was somehow able to ignore my legs and the problems I was having with the spasms. With my balance problems improved, I was becoming hopeful and excited about the future. In fact this was only the beginning of a long and difficult journey.

CHAPTER THREE

Early Days of the RDA (Side-Saddle)

I couldn't wait to get back to tell Sister Mary Joy about my new encounter, and had every hope that the RDA would know about this way of riding. Their response to my enthusiasm wasn't as positive as I'd hoped, but it was suggested that perhaps the Diamond Centre at Carshalton could cater to my needs. I made it my business to go and see them and hoped that they would take up my challenge; when all was said and done I wasn't looking to ride a camel. They tried to assist, but because of their inexperience with side-saddle we were unable to continue. Despite this setback, I continued to keep my weekly riding engagement at Wormwood Scrubs. I also made the long journey to Billingshurst each week to ride Waltzie. There I met a lovely friend called Rowena. For some time she had been riding another horse called Carrie, who also belonged to Cecily. I was envious of her because she rode with such ease; she really seemed to have her act together.

Unknown to me at the time, the secret of success lay in two things. The side-saddle must be the correct fit not only for the horse, but also for the rider. The rider should be able to sit in a balanced fashion, with both legs in a safe and comfortable position. If this is not the case, any rider trying to ride side-saddle for the first time will find it difficult to maintain balance, and possibly be put off the whole thing. Week after week, Rowena and I spent our time at Cecily's manége while she instructed us. One day she dressed me up in her beautiful habit and veiled bowler. Of course, Rowena already had all the gear and looked absolutely marvellous.

I should have looked the part, but I was still struggling to get my balance, especially in the left-leading canter, though Waltzie continued to look after me.

When a few months had flown by, Cecily told me that the SSA nationals were coming up in August. It didn't take me long to decide that this was something I must go to. There would be over a hundred entries from ladies and children and even the odd male rider – the best in the country and a number from overseas, making it an international competition. In those days the SSA nationals were held at the Malvern Showground.

My experience at the nationals was a revelation. I was in awe of the beautifully dressed ladies and their habits. They all looked so elegant. I was also delighted to find that there were stalls which had all the paraphernalia that anyone involved with horses needed. Looking around these stalls I met a young lady called Rebekah who was to become a lifelong friend. An enthusiast herself, she was willing to take me in hand. She soon became my dresser and a valued member of my team. My enthusiasm was bubbling over by this time. As I began to try on some of the items of dress I realised I had become absolutely committed to going down this pathway.

Following Rebekah's expert advice I bought a silk topper, one which had been owned by the previous president of the SSA. I also needed a bowler, as when one competes before midday more casual dress is appropriate. Silk topper and veil with silk cravat was for formal afternoon and evening wear. One needed to fully understand the correct dress code for this elegant sport. Habit and anything else that I would need that fitted me I bought. Silently I'd made up my mind that my goal was to be at the next year's competition myself, riding side-saddle. What enormous hurdle had I given myself? I didn't have a horse to ride or a saddle that would keep me safe.

I was desperate to begin enjoying this activity, but I was still badly disabled, having to use my wheelchair most of the time. At this stage I may not have had the full support of the RDA, but I certainly had the SSA on my side. I'd made a number of friends who were just as keen as I was and who were willing to do all they could to make it work for me.

When I returned from Malvern I heard from the Diamond Centre again. There was a vacancy that they could offer me and, apparently, they had found an instructor who could work with side-saddles. I was overjoyed! After being assessed by their physiotherapist I was accepted, but not for their advanced class, which was still full. The instructor of the class that I was placed in had no interest in side-saddle and soon made it clear to me that she wasn't going to teach it. I was back where I had started.

How fortunate I was to have a husband who was still encouraging me. Unselfishly he said, "All right, love, we'll have to go it alone."

Having realised that the side-saddle I'd been using at Cecily's was too big in the seat for me, I understood why I was still not comfortable, especially when trying to get a good balance at the canter. The first step was to find a side-saddle that would be right for me. Realising that side-saddles don't grow on trees – not even saddle trees – we had a challenge to discover where to start looking.

Again, chance came to the rescue in the shape of an advertisement in the SSA members' handbook. The advertisement was for a first-class saddler called Peter Smith. This master saddler operated out of a village called Shipton-under-Wychwood in Oxfordshire, which, as we soon learnt, was at the back of beyond. At the time we were living in Central London, so when I made the journey to see him I thanked my lucky stars that I could rely on my old Jaguar to do all this mileage. When all is said and done perhaps London is not the best place in the world to take up equestrianism.

Peter and his wife were very welcoming and took such a lot of trouble to try to help me find a suitable saddle. They had me try out every saddle in their collection, but they were all too big – long ways and width ways – and wrong in every other way. They eventually had to admit that it was going to be difficult to find a suitable saddle for me, but that they would continue to try.

After a few weeks Peter rang to tell me that he had found just what I needed, but at a price. The saddle was a fifteen-inch Owen in mint condition, owned by a collector who was reluctant to sell. This saddle was one of the smallest adult side-saddles ever produced. Another visit to remote Oxfordshire and another big hole in my bank balance resulted in me becoming the proud owner of one of the best side-saddles in the country. In the 1930s Owen's were the top makers of side-saddles, and they are still highly sought after.

I took my new acquisition to show Sister Mary Joy and hoped that we could use it on one of her ponies. She was willing to try, but had no experience herself, and it became obvious that it wasn't going to fit any of her horses. Yet another abortive attempt to get going on my side-saddle, but I refused to give up now!

Next I took it down to show Cecily. Bingo! The moment we put it on Waltzie my riding was transformed. For the first time I felt secure, and began to teach the old girl tricks that she'd never thought of.

On another day at Wormwood Scrubs, Sue Adams, whom we already knew to be an ally, suggested that I approach the South Buckinghamshire RDA group (South Bucks). She understood that they were a bit more specialised and had a trainer who might be willing to take me on.

I eagerly got in contact with Di Redfern, who was the owner

of the South Bucks group, and pleaded with her to consider me as a trial project. During my first visit I met Clive Milkins, the senior instructor and coach at South Bucks. He was a young man and a tough one to get to know. He had been responsible for coaching some of the riders who had just successfully competed at the 1996 Paralympic Games in Atlanta. This was the first time equestrians had been at the Paralympics, and Great Britain had come back home with all the medals.

Constantly seeking to aim higher, I began to dream of attending the next Paralympics as a competitor. Still more than three years away, it was to be held in my birthplace of Sydney, Australia.

CHAPTER FOUR

Big Monty

My first encounter with Clive Milkins was very friendly and helpful. He chose a horse called Big Monty for me to ride – a dear boy of just over sixteen hands, yet looking quite pony-like in his chestnut coat. Monty was quite willing to take my side-saddle, bless him. At the same time I met another rider who was riding side-saddle called Ann Williams. She told me that she had had a terrible accident when a tractor ran over her and she lost her legs in the process. She was doing brilliantly, I thought, and I thanked God that I at least had two legs!

Dear Monty proved to be a faithful friend, and our partnership was quite successful in competitions. We also gave displays from time to time to showcase how our way of riding helped individuals like Ann and myself cope with their difficult conditions. Soon after this South Bucks was able to fund and construct a very fine indoor school, along with a first-class arena. There was also a gallery for spectators, a room for lessons and a place to have tea. There were a number of returned Paralympic riders and Monty and I were very privileged to be part of the official grand opening day, where we gave a display of our riding. Bill prepared a lovely arrangement of music for Monty, which I rode to. It was an exciting day.

So far so good.

Now, Clive was at times not the easiest trainer to please or even get on with. His first evaluation of me was that I was overambitious, overconfident, and even over the top. He then added to this wonderful flattery by stating, along with some best-forgotten expletives, that I wouldn't last three weeks. Twenty years later, when I was still at it and working with other disabled riders, I reminded him of these memories in jest, over a lunch together. He apologised with a somewhat sheepish smile and quickly changed the subject.

At this point I was riding Monty each week and doing it with my side-saddle. I was also keeping up my sessions at Wormwood Scrubs. I was making noticeable progress with Clive, too, but it seemed that it would be impossible for me to compete with my side-saddle outside the RDA. These horses, including Monty, were in use constantly by disabled riders, either at the centre or at any of the RDA competitions. While I still had my sights on competitions with the SSA I also wanted to compete against able-bodied riders. In other words, in the real world!

Meanwhile, Sister Mary Joy asked me to act as a guinea pig at the examination day for the RDA instructors. I was, of course, delighted, and turned up looking spick and span. One of the examiners was Mrs Judy Gold, and after the exams were over I had an opportunity to put my problem to her. I explained that I was riding side-saddle and needed to find a horse that I could occasionally borrow for practice and take to competitions. She kindly suggested Suzanne's Riding School at Harrow Weald and soon afterwards my husband and I went to look it over.

Suzanne's was a very different set-up to anything I had seen before. It was a large commercial establishment in which a small RDA group formed a minor part. We were told that they had an instructor named Karen and by our good fortune she was taking a class at the time. When we met her she was delightful, friendly and encouraging, and she was also willing to let me do side-saddle. She introduced me to an elderly gentleman named Geeves, who was to be my mount. The following week the three of us got together and had a very enjoyable time. However, Geeves had seen it all before in his long life and had no intention of doing any more than he was paid to. I found this outlook increasingly frustrating as the weeks went by. I had, in fact, come to the conclusion that I was never going to make any real progress so long as I had to rely on riding-school horses. Sooner or later I would have to acquire one of my own.

To try to solve this problem I answered an advertisement from a lady in Hampshire who wanted help to exercise a horse. He was described as a quiet sixteen-hand Irish thoroughbred gelding, so I thought why not give it a try? When I told the lady that I rode side-saddle she seemed receptive. Once again, my long-suffering husband and I set off on another marathon drive, this time through East London to the country on the other side. I've said it before and I'll say it again – the Lord be thanked for my Jaguar!

Thankfully, the horse was lovely. His name was Duke and he was everything that one could wish for: gentle, kind and good-looking. He also had a nice action. His owner seemed pleasant enough, but the moment my husband saw her with Duke he noticed a strange reaction from the horse and warned me to be careful of both of them.

As there were no other facilities available, I had a very nice ride on Duke in a field. I then rode him back to the stable area, where I dismounted and his owner took him in hand. She was leading him, it seemed, to his stable, when he became frightened by a misplaced pile of stones and refused to go forward. We were horrified to see her hit him over the face with the reins. This, I guessed, was not the first time that poor Duke had felt the fury of his mistress; nor would it be the last, I thought! Altogether, she had four horses and I could see neurotic behaviour in all of them. The lady obviously had no idea about riding them or ensuring their well-being. I got out of there in a hurry!

How should I approach this problem? It was now a case of persuading Bill that I needed to have my own horse for the level of competition I was aiming for. What did we know about finding a horse that would be kind to me and trustworthy? Also it would have to take to side-saddle easily, and teach me all the skills that I would need to be a successful Paralympian rider. Not only that, I wouldn't be satisfied until I was good enough to compete against able-bodied riders.

Then there was the question of where to keep this horse? And who would look after it and me?

CHAPTER FIVE

Horse Hunting Begins

We started looking into every yard that kept horses professionally. After many, many phone calls I eventually talked to someone at the Priory Stables at Reigate. Its proprietor, Ian Duncan, was away at the time, but his assistant had assured me that Ian would return my call at the earliest opportunity. I'd heard this often enough and took little notice, especially as the other establishments I had spoken to had proved unhelpful.

We had kept in touch with Duke's owner and had tried everything we could think of to convince her to allow him to be brought under our care. Despite having more horses than she could cope with, she flatly refused to sell him. However, she was willing to consider some form of extended loan and, with Suzanne's permission, I put forward the idea of stabling him at Suzanne's establishment, at least on a part-time basis. All appeared to be moving forward smoothly until Duke's owner decided to visit the school on her own. There she met the secretary, a tough, business-minded, non-horsey woman. What happened I do not know as she refused to speak to us again. As for the riding school, I was told in no uncertain terms by the secretary that I was getting above myself, that Geeves was quite good enough for me, and that the whole idea of me owning my own horse was ridiculous. If I persisted they would have nothing to do with it or me. I suspect that the real reason behind this was their fear of being sued in case of an accident, but, as you can imagine, it was a devastating blow. It seemed that I was back where I started, with no horse and nowhere to go.

It was my husband who suggested a way out. "They aren't the only riding school in London," he told me. "I'll get the Yellow Pages and see what we can find."

He was right; within half an hour we had made a list of suitable establishments and I spent the next day putting my problems and propositions to every one of them.

My determination, rather than wavering, was sharpened by difficulties and the search for a horse continued. We bought every riding magazine we could get our hands on, marked each advertisement, then spent many hours phoning all over South-East England. The phone calls led to hundreds of motoring miles. It was a particularly cold winter and a number of the places we visited were awash in snow. We saw horses that were too big or too small, some that had tempers and some that were simply lacking in the necessary intelligence, but not one that was suitable. I was beginning to wonder if a pretty, docile, trainable sixteen-hand horse existed, or if such an animal was only a figment of my imagination.

Time was passing and I had set myself a target – to enter the RDA regional championships in May. It was now February and it seemed that I still had no horse, stabling facilities or instructor outside the RDA. I did, however, have a beautiful side-saddle and some very nice clothes, including specially made boots by Mr Schnieder. Schnieder Boots are the official supplier of 'Jack Boots' to Her Majesty the Queen's Lifeguards, Blues and Royals, which form her Household Cavalry. They also provide riding boots to the international Olympic equestrian teams of a number of countries, from Italy to Mexico. When I visited him in his New Bond Street studio he invited me to sit in a fine blue velvet chair and told me that the Queen herself had sat in the one that was beside me. What a charming, attentive and professional man he was, and I was most satisfied with my world-class footwear.

One evening the phone rang.

"This is Ian Duncan," said the voice. "Sorry I haven't called before, but I've had the flu."

Suddenly, light vanquished gloom!

That call lasted for well over an hour. Ian was fascinated by my intentions and assured me that he could help me. Furthermore, he bought and sold horses himself and promised that he would be able to find a suitable one for me before long.

The next day, full of hope and excitement, my husband, Bill, and I went down to see him. His expertise was immediately apparent and he questioned me closely on my experience and intentions. He showed me his horses and, though I didn't realise it at the time, I suspect that he was summing me up.

"All right," he said in the end, "I'll take you on." But he warned, "I'm going to work you very hard."

The whole experience began to resemble a large, unforgiving roller coaster. Meeting Ian was the crest of a wave, and the descent which followed immediately afterwards was both long and steep. Ian informed us that he was going away for a week's holiday and so we heard nothing from him. A week stretched into two, then three; still no contact. The riding-school horses seemed duller than ever and the May deadline loomed on the horizon. Frequent phone calls provided only an answering machine.

One evening the phone rang. It was Ian, full of apologies and explaining that he'd come down with another bout of flu. At last, after three weeks in the dark, we were back on track. Our search for a suitable steed resumed in earnest.

Meanwhile, we were still going to look at horses. The next one we saw was a brutally savage one called Mandy. A stable hand warned us to watch out for her back legs – a warning that was fully justified. Next there was a pretty Trakehner mare that I fell in love with immediately. When Ian came and looked at her he spotted instantly that she was far from fit or well. Next we met an ex-racehorse that had only two speeds – stop and flat out. It was unsuitable animal after unsuitable animal. I think this period was my most trying and difficult. Ian kept reassuring me that he would find me a good horse soon, but I was quickly losing hope. Like many equestrians, Ian was in the business of buying young horses, training them up and selling them. As the days wore on he asked again exactly how much we'd be willing to pay to get a horse that was just right.

"I don't know," I replied, leaving it up to his good judgement.

Finally, there was another phone call from Ian. "I've got a horse that you must come and see," he said.

I hotfooted it down to Reigate on my own; my husband was at work and, in any case, had insisted that his opinion of horses was almost worthless. What I would have done for an aeroplane at that moment!

CHAPTER SIX

Twinkle's Story and the First Dutch Nationals

Ian led me to a stable in which stood a rather plain-looking mare, freshly clipped and almost naked. I can't say that I was impressed, especially as the price was quite above my budget. Omaand Twinkle, for that was her rather comical name, seemed to have the same opinion of me. Twinkle was a six-year-old half-Irish draught and stood 16.1 hands. She wasn't what I would call pretty – fairly ordinary, in fact – but Ian assured me that she would do me proud. He did a lot of fast-talking, complimenting Twinkle on her pedigree and the expertise of her Irish breeders, and so on. Saddling her up, he took her for a ride around his school. I had to admit that, although she was badly out of condition, she did look better in action. Rather reluctantly I agreed to give her a try, and so we became her new owners.

The next challenge was getting my side-saddle to fit Twinkle. Ian had no experience of side-saddles so I had to call in a favour from one of my contacts at the SSA, Roger Philpot. He was an expert on everything to do with side-saddle and so I begged him for his assistance.

He agreed at once and was more than happy to drive down from Warwickshire to help me. He adjusted the saddle by redistributing the flock so that it was more comfortable and balanced on Twinkle. He then instructed Ian on the fitting of a side-saddle, before getting me mounted.

Twinkle didn't mind the saddle, but once again I was struggling to keep my balance. It soon became apparent that I would need to adjust the fit yet again and to do this we would have to consult another side-saddle expert, Michael Huline-Dickens. Michael came down from North London to Reigate and worked on fine-tuning my saddle, practically all day. My job was to keep him well fed and 'caffeinated'. He had me on and off Twinkle many times during the fitting process and the end result was very accurately calibrated. The difference it made to my seat was remarkable. Once again I was reminded of a lesson I had learnt once already – that the trick to riding side-saddle is mainly down to how well the saddle fits both the horse and rider.

Owning a horse comes with much responsibility. She had to have a whole lot of gear and so did I. Ian wrote me out a shopping list and suggested various tack shops and other emporiums where I could get what was required: rugs, head collars, field and exercise boots, bits and bridles, grooming paraphernalia and so on.

Twinkle was something of a novice herself, so Ian said that he would ride her regularly to get her fit and ready for me. Ian's manége faced a fairly busy road, with only a line of trees between the road and the arena. On many occasions the traffic would frighten Twinkle and several times I lost my balance and was thrown off, despite being locked into my side-saddle, where I assumed I would be safe. Later, I found out that Ian wanted a horse for jumping and, unbeknownst to me, had been jumping her when I wasn't around to see.

My partnership with Twinkle really began to warm up. The year was rushing by and my heart was still set on getting to the RDA nationals. These would be my first side-saddle nationals on my own horse and I was going to need all the help I could get. Firstly I needed to find someone who could provide Twinkle's transportation and hopefully be able to double up as groom when required. We met a lady named Sue who owned a suitable lorry and seemed very keen to assist me. Our first journey out together was to visit Cecily on her farm. Reigate to Billingshurst wasn't a particularly long journey, so David and Dorothy, old friends of Bill's, said that they would love to come and watch us. Dorothy was also a dab hand at video-editing.

On arrival, Cecily, being the super horsewoman that she was, gave Twinkle the once-over. She was fairly guarded about making any judgements, however. She was terribly kind though, and suggested we dress up for the occasion; that meant in her beautiful habit with bowler and veil. Of course, I needed a little help as the skirt – or apron, as it's called – is the strangest-looking garment that I have ever clapped eyes on. One has to look for the waist part, then do up some buttons on the left-hand side – what could be a placket in a ladies' skirt – and finally wrap half the blessed thing around one's right ankle, securing it around your boot. Hopefully this will cause the whole thing to hang beautifully and cover one's legs, saddle and half a horse.

By now, Sue had learnt to tack up Twinkle, and Rowena, already in costume, was there to give me a helping hand. Dressed and mounted, we entered the arena – Cecily's manége – to a round of applause from our considerable audience. Dorothy and David were very impressed at how elegant Rowena and I looked, for they had never seen riders dressed this way. As my confidence grew I decided to ask Twinkle for a canter. Here I must describe the difficulty for someone as disabled as I was to ask an inexperienced horse to lift into a canter, say on the right rein. This rein is not unlike the aid you would use if you were riding cross-saddle. But to do a left-leading canter, you only have a stick in your right hand to give your horse an aid to lift off on her right hind leg. These were still difficult moves for me to execute, but I attempted them all the same. Just at the crucial moment, a couple of very noisy birds decided to swoop from the thick line of trees which bordered the end of the school. Twinkle was spooked and took off, bucking along the full length of the school. Goodness me, what a frightening experience it was! Everyone panicked but had no idea what to do to help me. By the time Twinkle decided to pull herself together, I was pretty shaken up. I'd lost my balance and my dignity, but mercifully I'd stayed on. We didn't attempt any more cantering that day and it would be some time before I was confident and well balanced in all three paces – walk, trot and canter.

At this stage I was profiled by the RDA physiotherapist, Chris Meaden. Chris established the standard for profiling all para-riders. The scale of this profiling goes from I to IV, I being designated to the most disabled riders. My profile at this time was a II. This meant that when competing in any RDA events my test would only be done at walk and trot paces. My first and second RDA nationals, for which I had to qualify each year, were done at this level.

Two Australian riders came over to England to train and compete in an international friendly. We became fast friends and the girls asked me if I would join them in the Australian team; they needed a II profile to make up their contingent for the Sydney Paralympics. They were quite persuasive, but I could see that this might cause some problems, based on my membership and affiliation with multiple British equestrian organisations, and so I put the idea behind me. I was still improving in every way – physically and in my dressage performance. Therefore at my next profile assessment I decided to ride as a III.

I now required a serious coach and a specialist side-saddle instructor. I contacted a lady called Claire Lewis, the current Side-Saddle Rider of the Year and for the five years previously. It can't get any better than that, I thought. Claire very kindly said that she would come to my livery to teach me on Twinkle. This was some distance as she had to drive down from Ashford, in Kent.

I must take a moment here to express how kind and generous the SSA members were to me and to convey my gratitude for all the time and effort they put in throughout my riding and competing years. In fact, at that time the SSA hadn't worked with someone as disabled as I was and it was a big learning curve for them to get to grips with my additional needs.

The next step in qualifying for the RDA nationals was winning my class at the RDA regional championship. This was to be held at South Bucks in May and extra sessions were booked with Clive so Twinkle and I could get as much practice together as possible. Our hard work paid off! Twinkle and I won our grade-II class and were all set to compete at the nationals.

This year the nationals were hosted by Hartpury College, in Gloucestershire, for the first time. Di Redfern told me some years later that she had worked hard to get the venue switched to Hartpury, and I was lucky enough to compete there each year for the next twelve years.

The nationals at Hartpury were held on the second weekend of July each year, with the main competition taking place on the Saturday and Sunday. The preceding Thursday and Friday saw the world para-class and national squad competing in friendly competitions. This was before British Dressage (BD) took over the para-training sessions and competitions, which led to our world-class British team.

With the RDA nationals coming up in July, all training sessions had to be stepped up with Claire and Clive. We also required some financial assistance at this stage, and Bill was fortunate enough to acquire some sponsorship from the Arts Council. This helped, to some degree, in paying for Twinkle's training expenses.

At last it was time to make the trip to Hartpury for the weekend, although I wasn't competing until the Sunday. Sue transported Twinkle, as usual, but I realised that I required more professionals as grooms. Luckily one of the side-saddle grande dames, Peta Roberts, was an equestrian lecturer at Hartpury College. She kindly offered to find me a groom. Enter Jane Sauer, an equestrian student studying for her BSc in equine science and a capable rider. She was ideal as she could ride my horses in and warm them up for me. Little did I expect that Jane and, soon after, Wendy Anderson, also a student, would become two of my most loyal friends and work on my team for all my competing years. At Hartpury that year Jane rode Twinkle around to accustom her to the hurly-burly of a big competition. She clearly took to side-saddle too. We managed to get a fair place in our tests, but we were told by one para-trainer that Twinkle had some way to go if we wanted to be picked for Sydney.

Then in August we did our first side-saddle show at Malvern. We participated in a couple of novice classes as well as a costume class. I needed to hire a period costume this year, as there was no time to make one and as yet I was still inexperienced in creating my own.

It was also at these SSA nationals that we met and made long-term friends with two ladies called Charlotte and Christina, who came each year from Holland. They were the leading lights there and were planning to organise and open the Dutch national championship, which several of us British riders were invited to. This championship was to be held on 20 September – the year was 1998. As it happened, my dear friend Rebekah was to be married to Andrew that same weekend. Oh dear! Decisions had to be made and, with Rebekah's blessing, Bill and I decided to go to Holland.

Clive was delighted to join us and double up as groom and coach because the plan was that we were to be riding borrowed horses. Christina Meijer-Meijer owned a first-class resort and invited us to stay on-site in a beautifully arranged cabin. Driving from the airport in the dark was a bit fraught, as was finding her address, but thanks to Clive's observational skills we made it.

That evening, Bill left us to go and meet an old Dutch friend of his, whose main interest, like his, was aircraft.

The next morning we made our way to the venue and stables to meet our mounts for the competition. Clive, very quickly and efficiently, got to work on plaiting up and turning out the horse that I would ride. My side-saddle, which had travelled on the plane with us in a special compartment, was put on and, to our surprise, was not a bad fit. Now I had to mount and get out and do a warm-up. The other riders from Britain were also given mounts. They had attended the wedding the day before, so they had travelled overnight, still in full historical costume, to attend the event.

We entered several classes: a dressage, the equitation (which was called Best Riding Amazon) and the costume class. Most of us struggled to get any quality performance out of these horses, but it was a lot of fun. The lunch was a showpiece – "a barbecue to beat all barbecues," as Bill described it. During the break Clive and I spotted a lovely chestnut; it was the best looking animal we'd seen. We introduced ourselves and got talking to his owner, a young lady. She was very willing for me to ride him in the costume class and admired both my side-saddle and outfit. We weren't placed, but had an enjoyable time.

At the end of the day the last Dutch tradition we observed was 'tea'. This was provided mainly by the Brits' contribution of Dundee cake, Victoria sponges and other specialities. We had a wonderful time and Clive and I have been back – myself to compete, Clive to coach, and both to visit friends.

Back at the livery, Ian was pleasantly surprised that we'd

had such a good time and even brought back a few rosettes. Sadly, Twinkle didn't seem to be improving – at least not to the level I'd hoped for - and we started having some behaviour problems. An experienced vet was called and it seemed that Twinkle had some back pain. Maybe this was due to the side-saddle, or perhaps Ian had been asking too much when jumping her? She was only six years old, after all, and although I was only seven stone the side-saddle was quite weighty. If we were to rest Twinkle, then I wouldn't have time to reach the standard required to qualify for a trip to the Sydney games.

CHAPTER SEVEN

Hannah's Story

It became apparent that I required a more advanced horse at this stage and so all my friends were engaged to search for a suitable mount. We were recommended to a breeder of sporting horses called Debbie Johnston, a lady who trained her own horses and competed at a very high level in dressage. I gave her a ring and explained what I was hoping to do and where I was at with my riding experience. Debbie's horses were bred from Fleetwater Opposition, a Trakehner stallion who was a double gold medallist in eventing and a Prix St George dressage winner. Debbie was keen to show us one of his daughters, Opposition Varina, otherwise known as Hannah.

With some considerable excitement we drove down to Landford Common, near Salisbury, to meet Debbie and Hannah. As soon as I laid eyes on Hannah it was love at first sight – not always a wise start! She was a beautiful shining black, 16.1 hands, and ten years old. She had had an interesting history too. At the age of five she had been bought by a lady wanting to compete with her in dressage. Sadly, the new owner developed cancer and was too ill to ride her. Debbie had kept Hannah and rode her from time to time to keep her healthy and in shape. Eventually her owner died, which is why Hannah was now up for sale. The asking price was far more than we could realistically afford, but, after a great many trial rides and assurances that she would have a lovely life and home, a more suitable sum was agreed upon. Debbie's husband kindly offered to transport Hannah to the new yard where she would be living from now on. Before we could make any further decisions, Hannah first needed to be looked over by a vet. We chose a local vet, from an established practice that specialised in equine care, to carry out a full examination.

We waited with bated breath for almost a week; then, at last, the phone call came. She had passed with flying colours and when we saw the certificate the examiner's remarks stated that she would be suitable for dressage with a partially disabled rider.

Hannah had been schooled to medium-level dressage by Debbie, though she hadn't yet competed. In short, she was very inexperienced for a ten-year-old. Though I was still a novice, I was delighted to discover that she immediately responded well to my aids and voice. Now it was important that I developed a balanced seat for side-saddle and that Hannah carried herself forward and into a soft contact on the bit, through the reins. She needed to strengthen her back and hindquarters while remaining supple at the same time. These skills are essential when schooling a dressage horse, and we would spend forever perfecting them. Poor Twinkle needed to be put out to grass, as she needed a well-deserved rest, and kind Sue took her on.

It was not easy to find a suitable yard to take Hannah. I needed someone who understood how to keep a quality dressage horse. They needed to administer the correct diet so that she would not get overheated and have more energy than I could manage. At the same time she needed to build some muscle and have enough 'sparkle' for the job.

I needed good surfaces to ride on and above all an indoor school so that I could ride in rain, hail or shine in comfort. We visited several livery yards in the area and eventually found all our needs were catered for at All Manor Park Livery and

Stables in Chipstead, Surrey. Jenny Webb was the commercial manager and she was very willing to take us on. Hannah would be on partial/full livery and have a lovely stable and plenty of fields to roam about in. There was an excellent manége and an indoor school. I would be able to park my car right next to her stable and carry out a great deal of her care myself, including grooming and, with a little help, tacking-up. My trusted side-saddle and tack travelled with me each day on the two-and-a-half-hour round trip from London.

Debbie had thoughtfully written a covering letter which came with Hannah. Looking back at her remarks, they read:

> I know you will be a great partnership, but please forgive Hannah if she is a little confused at first. She is so used to Landford Common, but I am sure she will settle in very quickly with T.L.C.
>   Much love
>   Debbie.

For most of her life up to this point she had been free to do her own thing, but now we needed a fairly strict routine if we were going to make it in the highly competitive world of dressage. She was not the easiest of horses to work with. At times she could be very sweet and affectionate, but she had some difficulty in managing mood swings; on other occasions she would bite and kick out with ears back and an expression in the eyes and face that said, 'Kill.'

I quickly learnt that her temperament must be understood and managed if we were going to trust each other. I had a hunch that she was an insecure animal who needed a firm but loving owner, and that was what I tried to practise.

We urgently needed to return to South Bucks to get our training back on track with Clive. Fortunately, Sue was still able to be our transporter and groom. Clive was keen to try Hannah out, and I thought he rode her very well. He then wanted to do it side-saddle – good for Clive! – and in no time had her working equally well with both types of saddle. In fact she took to Clive in a really big way and started to follow him around like a Monty Roberts horse. He bribed her into 'bending', using apples and carrots – a method I've continued to use to this day, before and after riding. When I got on I had a bit more trouble getting her into a relaxed outline, but Sue, Bill and Clive all thought our first session together went fairly well. We all hoped that the care she was receiving at the livery would be beneficial to our progress. When the time came to go home, Sue and I had a real struggle getting Hannah into her travelling boots, tail bandages and coat – she was quickly turning to her 'bad' side. Then she decided that she wasn't going up into the lorry.

Clive was unimpressed by this performance and thought that she was showing dangerous behaviour for a horse meant for a disabled rider. He stepped in and, without much further ado, used his authority to help Sue get her into the horsebox. Hannah had a lot going for her – she was very pretty and had great paces – but her temper tantrums would need to be controlled if we were to get the best out of her.

I quickly learnt that when her ears went back and she gave me a threatening look there was no point smacking her or getting too involved with an argument – she was always going to have the last word. But occasionally she would go over the top and really test me to react. So I would raise my voice, stamp my foot and throw a brush (or anything else I could get my hands on) to the ground – in other words throw a tantrum to the same level of stress as she was displaying. This usually got her attention and distracted her from her inappropriate game. My outbursts used to amuse some of the liveries, but I think they thought it a fairly original way of treating bad behaviour.

There was a training week and talent-spotting coming up at Hartpury College and we were invited to attend by Jane

Goldsmith, now the late Jane Goldsmith, who trained the top para-team. I was excited to take part and so I contacted Peta Roberts to let her know the news. She was very willing to give me extra coaching because of my side-saddle needs. We were still a new experience for trainers and judges. Someone aiming at high-level dressage while riding side-saddle, as well as being disabled, was quite a challenge for them. But that's what I thought was the best route to success, and by now I was quite committed to it.

These training days were a rich experience and Hannah seemed to enjoy herself. She began to loosen up and her 'medium trot' was her party piece. We had impressed Jane sufficiently to suggest that Peta should be my contracted trainer. Very luckily, both Jane and Peta were Fellows of the British Equestrian Federation, an affiliate of the International Federation for Equestrian Sports (FEI). This was a very high honour indeed. Now Hannah and I needed to prove ourselves worthy of being picked for the national squad. We needed to compete as often as we could in side-saddle events in order to prepare ourselves for the National Side Saddle Show.

Life became fairly hectic – my regular RDA training with Clive; weekly lessons with Claire Lilley, my new coach; journeying to Hartpury to practise with Peta; and keeping up my part-time job as a college lecturer to help pay for all this.

Going to the side-saddle nationals this year meant that I had to make a historical costume, and one that would enhance our appeal. Bill, being a historian, was helpful in choosing a picture which I would copy. He found a beauty: an equestrian portrait by Antoine-Jean Gros of Queen Catherine of Westphalia, wife of Jerome Bonaparte, the brother of Emperor Napoleon. Competing in these classes was to be my forte, now and for many years to come.

This year, Valerie Millwood, Area 8's long-time chairperson and well-known judge and trainer, was approached by the

BBC to choose a rider to be filmed for a documentary they wished to do for their *Countryfile* programme – I was chosen. We were followed from class to class by a cameraman and the BBC producers. They were most interested in the historical-costume class that I was preparing for. I was being helped into my costume in the stable while Hannah was getting her elaborate gear on and saddled up. Fortunately, everyone knew their role as the tricky business of getting me mounted was all being filmed. They wanted to see the way my costume was presented to be judged, and, as fortune had it, I won the class.

I was then escorted back to our stable, still with cameras rolling. At the stable, the girls had laid out a white sheet on the ground so that when I dismounted my tremendously long dress, with yards of real ermine around the bottom frill, wouldn't get soiled. Hannah had decided that she wouldn't have anything to do with setting foot on a white surface and 'took off' sideways with me still on board, quickly pursued by Jane. After some firm persuasion she eventually decided to behave herself and I was carefully helped to dismount with dress and all still intact. Some careful editing was done before we saw the television programme we were featuring in.

One day, while attending a training event at South Bucks with Jane Goldsmith, a young rider turned up with his pony. He was introduced to me as Lee Pearson. Severely disabled, he impressed everyone present and, though he knew very little, if anything, about dressage, one could see that his horse sense and riding skills were out of the ordinary. I was told, off the cuff, that his parents bought him a pony, not a pram.

Our training sessions at the school would again coincide, and this time Lee was given dear old Monty to ride.

"How do you get this one going?" he asked me.

Now, with all the times I had ridden this 'dear boy' I should have been able to give some useful advice, but I hesitated in case I got pulled into something that I might regret at a later date.

A while later, a question came again: "How do you get a canter?"

Now I was a bit bemused as I was sure that Lee had already worked all this out, but perhaps he was testing me – what fun! Although this young rider was severely disabled, he eventually competed nationally, internationally and as a Team GB dressage rider in Paralympic Games going back to Sydney in 2000. He won more gold medals than he could decorate his house with! So, you see, everyone has a beginning.

There were many more of these training days and I made friends with several other para-riders. Eventually I would go on to became a regular in the national squad and compete internationally. To this end, the extent of my disability needed to be re-examined. I had to be profiled by two physiotherapists, one of whom had to be of another nationality. These examinations weren't the most pleasant for me – or any of the other riders, I imagine. These two professionals had to make certain that no rider was able to fake any weakness. In so doing, we were put through some pretty painful contortions. My results were similar to my original profiling – just over the border into being a III profile.

By this point, and thanks to all the help I'd had, my riding skills had really improved. My confidence and balance enabled me to compete at all three paces, including canter, and I was working towards a medium level in my tests. Hannah was quite able to work at this level when she put her mind to it, and when she was at her best we were a great team.

In those days, back in the 1990s, all national and international competitions were still done on borrowed horses. If you owned a horse, it would be given to another rider to use in a separate class from you. Very often, I would be given the biggest horse in the stables. I was never quite sure of the thinking behind this; it seemed that for a horse to take side-saddle it had to be large, even though I was only seven stone.

During an international friendly, a situation arose where they couldn't find a suitable horse to carry my saddle; it just didn't fit any of them. They brought a 17.2-hand horse for me to try, but once again my little saddle was far too small for him. As this event was happening at Hartpury College, Peta was on hand to assist me. She knew of a beautiful advanced dressage horse called Shucks and managed to persuade the owner to loan him to me. Peta used to compete on Shucks too, and I couldn't believe my luck. He was very special and I was a bit nervous that now I might be 'over-horsed', as the saying goes.

During the warm-up he tried to get away from me when I went into a canter, so I just turned him into a corner to stop him in his tracks. I wasn't going to have any argument with this bright one; nor could I match his strength if he decided to continue. We entered the arena to do my test. All seemed well – the going seemed good. I came up to a change of rein at the canter, which should have been a simple change – canter, walk three to five strides, canter – all done effortlessly and smoothly. As we came to the spot where this movement should take place, Shucks took matters into his own stride and did a magnificent flying change, a movement way above what was needed and that I had asked for. We'd just thrown away quite a few marks, depending on how generously or otherwise the judges viewed the manoeuvre. Already I was feeling a little nervous about our performance, and yet we would have to do a mirror of that movement on the other rein. I had just a few seconds to consider how I was going to organise the next one; but the more I tried to collect him and myself together, the more he tried to pre-empt my commands. He was really only trying to be helpful. Right on the spot where he should have been doing several walking strides, up he went into the air, his hind legs drawing underneath him – and bingo, another flying change! Despite these faux pas I thought that we had done a nice test.

After the class had finished one of the judges came over to me and congratulated us on our beautiful flying change. However, when we got our scores they told a very different story – we had thrown away many marks and were several places behind the winner. Well, it was a lesson well learnt – that one can be lucky enough to be riding a clever horse, but that the horse shouldn't be teaching its rider in a competition.

CHAPTER EIGHT

A Side-Saddle Experiment and Display

Jenny, at All Manor, had been very supportive and interested in all my side-saddle activities. One afternoon she suggested that I give a display for all the other liveries and their friends. 'What a worthwhile challenge!' I thought, and began to plan an event that would give others an insight into the skills and benefits of the sport. Rather than just having the one rider, I thought we'd have a greater impact if I invited other side-saddle enthusiasts to join the fray. I decided that my first guinea pig should be Claire Lilley, my current trainer. Claire was classically trained in Germany and the UK and I was very fortunate to have her experience on my team. Her horse, Amadeus, was young and inexperienced and I thought he would make an excellent candidate for my experiment. Claire loved the idea and was very happy to participate. My initial idea began to grow and I decided that we needed more horses to make up a quadrille. It wasn't long before all the All Manor horses were being offered up eagerly. I soon realised that I needed some serious assistance if I were to make this a successful venture. I phoned Claire Lewis, our side-saddle rider par excellence, and my dear friend Rebekah, and suggested they join me for the display. They were both up for the challenge, and furthermore it was decided that we should perform in historical costumes to take it all to another level.

I gave each rider a ground plan of the choreography before

the day, so each one had a fair idea how it would all fit in. Very often, it was useful to walk it out without the horses and this could be quite fun. Not being very mobile in my wheelchair, someone would have to step in and take my place on foot. Then I would call out all the movements from the sideline. It became even more amusing when everyone wanted to practise going through the movements to the music. As two feet can't perform anything like four feet, usually things would get into a horrible muddle. It was always best if you could run through the whole event mounted, even if it needed to be done a few times to get it right.

On the day there was a considerable level of excitement, with horses being washed and groomed in the hope of being a side-saddle candidate.

Claire and Rebekah arrived with an assortment of side-saddles and a wonderful wardrobe of costumes. Claire had some lovely nineteenth-century outfits – one for her to wear and one for Claire Lilley, my trainer. Rebekah, being well versed in competing in costumes, brought one of her most spectacular ones – a copy from a picture of an Arabian princess mounted on an Arab horse whose bridle was studded with jewels. I would wear a costume made for Hannah, taken from a George Stubbs portrait of *The Countess of Coningsby in the Costume of the Charlton Hunt*.

Saddles were tried out on various horses and expectations were rising. The best fit was given to Amadeus, and we also managed to kit out two others satisfactorily. We had our quadrille, and decided to use the music Bill had prepared to use at our French championships. It was George Frideric Handel's *Cuckoo and the Nightingale*, and it fitted the occasion perfectly. It had a long 'trot' and a short 'canter' that should match these horses' paces.

We now had all four horses ready and fitted with side-saddles.

It took a bit of patience and skill to get them happily going into a practice run. Each rider did her own freestyle, before grouping together for a run-through of the choreography and finally one to the music. All this was done to the amazement of our audience, for everyone had got into the whole mood of the experiment.

The time came to get horses and riders into their costumes for our performance. By this point it was the middle of the afternoon and we were lucky enough to be enjoying a lovely, warm sunny day. Claire and Rebekah were delighted with their mounts, and Amadeus had taken to it most remarkably.

The music started and I led us in single file down the centre line of the arena. At the far end was a row of thick fir trees. All four horses knew this and had ignored them up until now. Suddenly, Hannah stopped as if she'd seen a tiger, and refused to continue. Rebekah's horse veered off in another direction and, as he did so, Amadeus's eye was distracted by the bright colours of her voluminous skirt. It was all too much for him and he went straight up in the air, 'airs above the ground'. It was utter mayhem while the music rolled on.

After an abortive start we regrouped and managed to get through the performance without any more drama. The audience thought it was a lovely performance and wanted a rerun. Jenny had also invited a journalist from the local newspaper; photos were taken and a story of the event was published in both the local news and various equine magazines.

A remarkable thing was said by Claire Lilley: "If I hadn't been riding side-saddle I'd have been thrown off Amadeus!"

Overall the day was a success. It had been a lot of fun and a big learning experience for everyone involved. It ended with a tea party and Rebekah's beautiful costume got a closer inspection from many admiring attendees.

Our next event was at Wormwood Scrubs. It was coming up

to Christmas time and Sister Mary Joy planned a show. I was thrilled to be invited to do a little display with Hannah as part of the entertainment. I decided to do a short piece that Bill had already arranged the music for, and I would once again wear my Countess of Coningsby habit. I asked Claire Lewis and Rebekah to come and assist me. Claire's mother, Valerie, who was very supportive of Claire, came along as well. Sue transported Hannah to Wormwood in good time and Claire graciously warmed Hannah up for me. It was a desperately cold, rainy night and we had to get from stable to indoor school without Hannah or myself getting soaked through. Hannah needed her thick woolly rugs on to keep her warm and dry, and I was taken over in my wheelchair with a mackintosh and umbrella to protect me from the elements. Such are the difficulties that one has to face when it comes to British winters. Claire had done a marvellous job in the warm-up and Hannah seemed to have a sense of the occasion of the evening. The music began and we did a great job of synchronising our transitions. Some of the arena had been taken up by a large chunk of the audience and we hadn't had a chance to practise in the limited space. All went well, and when it came to the final salute I was very pleased with our performance.

Rowena and Rayna on Waltzie and Carrie.

Cecily Friar and Rayna on Waltzie and Carrie.

Twinkle's first win at Wormwood Scrubs – Desi Dillingham, chief executive of BD.

Twinkle's first side-saddle nationals, with Rayna in a borrowed historical costume.

Rayna and Big Monty at South Bucks RDA with Rayna's own new side-saddle.

Ian Duncan and Rayna – meeting Twinkle for the first time.

Martina's first RDA nationals at Hartpury.

Dawn, Rayna's first palomino when she was nine years old.

Martina at her best.

Rayna and Henry, borrowed on the day, winning the historical-costume class at the SSA nationals with their interpretation of the Duchess of Gordon as Chief of the Gordon Highlanders.

Left to right: Claire Lilley on Amadeus, Rayna on Hannah, Claire Lewis on a livery horse, and Rebekah Marks-Hubbard on a livery horse, doing our quadrille to music.

Beethoven.

Rayna heading for the 'turnout' class with Jane Sauer, her groom.

*Teasle and Rayna competing at the SSA 25th Anniversary
Nationals, 1999.*

*Grooms Jane and Wendy
with Monty Roberts,
winning at the nationals.*

*Teasle and Rayna in her Duchess of Berry costume
at the SSA nationals, 1999.*

Rayna winning at the French nationals, awaiting the medals ceremony, but her wheelchair would not fit on the podium.

Madame Carole de Chabot (far left), Paula Keely (far right), Rayna and friend.

The British team at the French International SSA Championships, 16 June 2002.

Bill and Rayna winning at the RDA Championships, 1997.

*Barbarella and Rayna in our controversial summer costume, styled on
an Edwardian linen outfit with boater and veil.*

Clive and Rayna doing their pas de deux on Mr Custard and Barbarella.

Pairs with Becky on Charlie and Rayna on Barbarella.

Rayna in her Duchess of Mar costume on Barbarella.

Dressage to music on Barbarella at the SSA nationals, 2001.

Barbarella and Rayna in France in costume as Queen Marguerite of Spain, performing in a temperature of around 40°C.

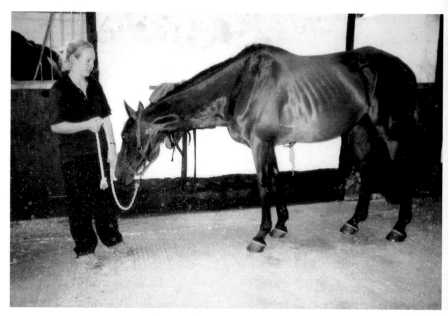

Rescued Star in poor health.

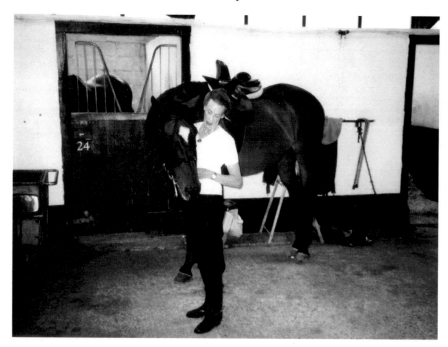

Star, now ready to be ridden.

CHAPTER NINE

Hannah Is Taken to Liphook

One morning Jenny phoned with the sort of news no one wants to hear. She had found Hannah having a colic attack and a vet had been called and was on the way. I threw some clothes on and set off on my hour's journey from London through the peak-hour traffic. I had been most fortunate thus far in my equine career never to have a horse develop colic, so this would be a new experience for me. By the time I arrived the vet had already given her the appropriate medication, but it hadn't helped her symptoms or her pain. This was turning out to be a serious worry – she urgently needed to be taken to the Liphook Equine Hospital. There it was decided that she needed surgery immediately and I was politely informed that there would be no need for me to hang about there. Once the operation was over I was told that I could visit her. She was still in intensive care when I arrived, sedated and with a drip in place. She was actually lying down, so I sat down beside her and placed her head on my lap. She seemed to appreciate the comfort of my presence and affectionate stroking. I came to visit her each day for as long as she needed me.

The surgeon explained to me that she had huge holes in her omentum, the membrane that covers and protects the whole gut. This could have happened when she was a foal or maybe as a result of a worm infestation, though I'm sure she had the best care in her younger years. It was deduced that this could have been part of the reason for her mood swings; she may have been experiencing constant belly-gripping pains. I just wanted her to recover swiftly and feel better.

Her discharge day came and I was given strict instructions for her care, all written out by the surgeon on Liphook Equine Hospital headed paper. There was to be no guessing here, and I had to have the cooperation of Jenny for her complete recovery.

The orders were as follows – eight weeks' box rest, then four weeks' walking out regularly, and convalescent diet for her feed. We were to contact our local vet to remove the stitches and staples at the appropriate time and there would be follow-up visits to the hospital after three months. All this seemed perfectly reasonable and we didn't predict being presented with any serious problems. Unfortunately, Hannah, as you'll remember, had spent most of her life in a field pleasing herself. She considered this to be a good life and wasn't having any of this box rest. We tried sedation to make it more palatable, but that just made her more crazy to get out. Her behaviour was very worrying and our attempts at calming her down were to no avail. We were at our wits' end when Jenny suggested that she might be better in a little 'corral'. She went to a lot of trouble to build one in a position where Hannah could see her friends in the field, while restricting her enough to keep her from harming herself. However, Hannah somehow managed to jump the fence, bringing the whole thing down, and galloped away to join her friends, doing untold damage to herself and the fence in the process. We now had a horse with a massive herniated wound and all her innards hanging out. The local vet thought that her wounds could be repaired, but the situation was dire, and my immediate concerns lay in how to deal with her uncontrollable behaviour. We had some very troubling discussions and realised that the risks were high whatever we did. In the end the decision was left with me. Hannah was clearly not happy being safely nursed back to health, and no one had a clear and practical way forward to offer her. God help me – Hannah had got her way, but had got it wrong if she was going to survive this. Unfortunately, horse reasoning and human reasoning don't always coincide.

Bill was most concerned for her, though it didn't seem that we could find a solution to keep her happy. We were beginning to think the worst. Could we carry on or not? Again the vet from the Gayton Group was called. She was very understanding of the problems we were facing, yet in the end the decision was left with me to come up with some humane way of dealing with Hannah. Her well-being was at stake and I had to do the right thing for both of us. She was a most unusual and difficult case and there was really only one way out. I asked myself over and over, "Is there any other way?" but in the end I knew the best decision for all concerned was for her to be euthanised. My sense of grief and loss was palpable. She had become a most unusual friend and companion and I would miss her dearly. There was no time for any more post-mortem, however; I had to let Debbie, Jane, Wendy and all the others know the sad news. Once again, all of my plans and goals seemed to be in jeopardy! How could she be replaced and in a hurry?

Looking back over the three years, we'd had a full and exciting career together. Though woefully cut short, it had grown from strength to strength. We had been invited to give many displays to show the benefits of side-saddle riding. There were the more specialised events in historical costumes, all done to such lovely music. We'd done a few cabaret evenings at pony clubs, Wormwood Scrubs, etc. We had qualified for RDA and SSA nationals each year and our dressage levels and scores had improved greatly. We'd also competed in the national para-dressage squad internationally. Now I had to have a rethink – where does one go from here?

Despite her oversized attitude and nasty temper, which I had to humour and at times struggled with, she had won my heart and soul. She was simply a beautiful creature and would be sorely missed.

Little did I know the answer to my dilemma was in the pipeline, though still some distance away.

CHAPTER TEN

Teasle to the Rescue

Once again, the hunt was on for a replacement horse. My next session with Clive was already booked and I would be back with Monty. I had tears that day and for some time afterwards, but Clive was very understanding and sympathetic. He told me about a horse and its owner that he knew. The horse, Barbarella, had a successful pony-club jumping career and was an elementary-level dressage competitor. Right now, though, she was recovering from an injury and was also in foal, so she would need some time off before she would be ready to come back to work. However, Clive's enthusiasm about the horse's assets made me prick up my ears, despite the time it would take before she would be free to continue a career in competing. Meanwhile I needed to find a replacement if I was to keep riding.

Once again, fortune came to my rescue in the form of a horse called Beethoven. He had been a very successful competitor at the Barcelona Olympics and was now owned by a young lady called Sarah Carter, a stunning junior rider for the SSA. I thought Beethoven and his rider were quite simply the bee's knees – they had it all.

Sarah had just left school and would soon be off to Cambridge University to study pedagogy. Her mum, Rosalyn, asked me if I'd like to ride her horse for the year while Sarah was away. She wanted to keep Beethoven fit and in form just in case Sarah wanted to resume her riding at some point. What an invitation and marvellous luck! Rosalyn was also willing to let me continue his schooling, and she offered to assist with my coaching.

That was a fabulous year. We went to all the SSA shows and events. These included the annual show at Sotheby's country estate at Billingshurst and a grand polo event at Cowdray Park, where we did a display and quadrille. I had a wonderful time and these were such high-profile events! But Beethoven had a dark secret which I hadn't been aware of up to this point. One day, while helping the grooms prepare him for a show, he took off from the stable at a gallop, yanking me along with him. I had been holding him by his head collar to keep him still for the girls to plait up his mane. This was a naughty prank that he played on anyone he thought he could get away with. My right shoulder was painfully strained and I had real difficulty getting into my costume when the time came. That's horses for you!

Beethoven couldn't be ridden for my RDA events; Rosalyn was happy for me to ride him at SSA ones, but wasn't keen on the additional red tape involved at the RDA. However, my luck was still going strong – back at Hartpury College, Peta and Jane were working behind the scenes to find me an appropriate co-competitor. Jane knew of a grey horse called Teasle, and I gathered that between the two of them they were able to persuade Teasle's owner to allow me to compete on her for the year. She was a sweet 16.1-hand mare and was so kind and gentle. With this new partnership I was able to compete in the 1999 RDA nationals and SSA nationals. And there was something else about Teasle which inspired me – being a 'grey', and almost white in colour, made her a perfect match for me to make a very special historical costume. I had pictures of the famous French manuscripts – *Les Très Riches Heures du Duc de Berry* – and in particular the beautiful equestrian May scene at the Hôtel de Nesle from 1410. This featured a white horse ridden by the Duchess of Berry.

"That's the costume to take to the French nationals!" was Bill's remark!

Teasle took to side-saddle, costumes and everything, and loved it all. We had a very successful and fun year, but sadly it soon came time to return her to her owner.

CHAPTER ELEVEN

Barbarella's Story

Again I was horseless and unable to compete. Then, out of the blue, I got the news from Di and Clive that Barbarella was now fit, well and looking for a good home on a permanent loan. They thought that she would be just right for me, although I was rather unenthusiastic about taking on a nineteen-year-old mare that had been out of work for three years to have a foal. Clive, though, told me that I'd be stupid not to try her. "It's not going to cost you anything and you can always send her back if she's no good."

He had a point, so I arranged for her to be delivered to my livery at All Manor.

I signed an agreement with Cathy Fenn, the owner. Barbarella's passport identified her as a 15.3-hand Welsh part-bred, with a freeze mark to protect against theft. The only stipulation in the agreement was that I wouldn't be jumping her, and that suited me just fine.

Jenny put her in an isolation stable for forty-eight hours, just in case she had come with an infection that could be passed on to the other liveries.

At first glance, I was not impressed. Barbarella was straw-coloured, somewhat shabby-looking and had a rather hangdog expression. I got the impression that she was no more impressed with me than I was with her. A few days' acquaintanceship, however, suggested that she was worth persevering with. She was gentle and anxious to please – a complete contrast to Hannah.

At this point, everything was interrupted by our moving from London to Portsmouth. I managed to find a livery yard not too far away from our new location and, between spells as a builder's labourer, took Barbarella's schooling seriously in hand.

I took great care to provide her with a strict daily routine and appropriate diet. With this in hand she began to blossom: her colour deepened, she muscled up and she really started to look very pretty. She showed herself to be intelligent and willing, and soon developed into a real companion. After six months I felt that she was ready to try a low-grade competition. The season started slowly, but before long she began to shine. Our first success was winning our class at the Southern RDA Regional Championships, which ensured we qualified for the nationals. At the nationals we came third in our class and fourth in the grade-III kur, with percentages in the sixties and encouraging remarks from the judges.

Next up came the SSA nationals, where to my utter astonishment we won the open novice dressage and the historical-costume class. We also came third out of a class of twenty-five in the freestyle kur, which was ridden at elementary level. Again, our marks were very encouraging.

The weather in August for the SSA nationals can vary enormously and this year had decided to be scorching-hot. I had previously been asked if I would design a summer habit for just this kind of weather. I had gone to a lot of trouble to research the subject during conversation with Joyce Bellamy, who was an expert costume historian and a member of my Area 8 side-saddle group.

I designed and tailored this habit in an Edwardian style, using off-white linen with a boater and veil, inspired by a newspaper article and pictures of the times.

I'd entered the mature riders' class for ladies over a certain age and decided this would be the occasion to wear my new summer habit. As I entered the ring we caused a sensation. We were quickly apprehended by two stewards, who were concerned about whether wearing a boater was permitted, traditional or even safe. It seemed that I would need the judges' permission to continue in the class. Miss Elizabeth Turner, a dear friend, was happy to let us continue, and we were well placed in spite of the controversy we had started. I had many compliments and a representative from Caldene, who are outstanding tailors of riding wear, was impressed enough to consider making a similar lightweight habit.

Next came a big adventure: Carole de Chabot, who was at the forefront of side-saddle riding in France, invited me to compete in their first side-saddle international competition. Carole was an English lady who had married a French aristocrat named Philippe, and we were invited to see their château. Carole came to our British SSA Championship each year and brought some of her French riders with her. There was Laurence, Emmanuelle, Fabienne and Pierre. Their association was called La Pirouette Equitation. The competition to which I had been invited was being held at the national stud at Le Lion d'Angers. This venue was just a few miles north-west of Le Cadre Noir de Saumur, the École Nationale d'Equitation, a classical academy of riding where they famously performed 'airs above the ground'. The show was over a long weekend, so we decided we would need to go for at least four days in order to recover from our journey and get accustomed to the hot climate.

My good friend Paula Keely had also been invited, and we were both very excited to accept. Paula kindly transported Barbarella in her horsebox along with her chestnut mare, Alpha. We would sail by night from Portsmouth to Cherbourg, and we arranged for Jane and Wendy to accompany us. Paula's lorry was large enough to take all the feeds and tools the horses would need while we were there. Bill and I drove in convoy across the beautiful French countryside, with all my valuable tack and several habits and costumes in the back of the car. We used his Vanden Plas Princess as it was more comfortable to travel in and had good space for all the gear.

We reached the gates of the Haras, an establishment run by the National Stud of France, and we were met by M. Boutolot, the director, who led us through the beautiful grounds to the stable block. This was palatial, like everything else in the Haras, centred on a lovely old château. It is one of the finest settings we have competed in.

It was lunchtime and the horses – Alpha, twenty-two years old, and Barbarella, twenty years old – needed rest, feed and watering. Towards the cool of the evening we just had to have a hack around these magnificent grounds.

It was suggested that we form a quadrille as part of our performance at the show – half English, half French. I prepared a ground plan for the four of us to ride to and Bill provided the music. Naturally, we all performed in costume.

Paula and I had some idea of what we were supposed to do, but Linda, who was Paula's friend and came as her groom, had only tried side-saddle for the first time the week before, and we didn't know what Carole, who was the fourth member, could do either. Even the music – Bill's department – was second-hand, as he had had no time to work out something new. The next morning was spent getting the quadrille together. We used the 'marching method' first, i.e. me shouting out instructions from my wheelchair and using my stick to point in the directions that everyone should be going. This usually caused much laughter from everyone looking on, and I suspect that Bill was one of them. It became even more chaotic once we got mounted, yet with several slow runs-through, gradually getting it up to speed, it began to take shape.

In the competition our quadrille was last into the arena. Some of the French teams had put up very attractive performances, especially one group who all wore matching dresses. However, we didn't disgrace ourselves and everyone seemed to be in the right place most of the time. Imagine our utter astonishment when we were called out at the prize-giving as the winners! Paula won the advanced dressage and I came second. In the concours the position was reversed – I won in my Duchess of Berry costume and Paula came second in her yellow eighteenth-century costume. This event is organised quite differently to ours. There are several judges sitting on a dais and each competitor rides in and salutes them. They are then given a microphone and describe their costume to the judges and, through a loudspeaker, to the spectators. They then give a little freestyle display. In my case, this was fairly tame as it was too dangerous to canter in a skirt trailing nearly to the ground. Paula, however, did a super show, making Alpha dance through a series of flying changes to such effect that she had to give an encore.

The French had gone to a lot of trouble with the beautiful trophies and prizes that they presented to the winners. I still wear with pride the Hermès scarf and watch I won. The perfume has long been used up, but I have a magnificent bronze statue of a horse in my conservatory taking pride of place among a few other riding ornaments. Before we set off for home we were able to visit Le Cadre Noir de Saumur and see an equine performance. Our bed and breakfast was run by an English lady by the name of Madame May. We were well looked after and it was hoped that we would come again. Altogether, our visit to France was a great success.

CHAPTER TWELVE

Hard Training in Earnest

In 1998 I was invited to attend training days with the national squad. The selection criteria for international competitions for riders with disabilities were rather difficult to meet:

- Riders must have had considerable competition experience.
- They must be obtaining a minimum score of 58% in said competitions.
- Selectors must be familiar with the standard of the international competition to be entered.
- The selectors must have seen riders compete in national or international competitions to be certain of their competence.
- Riders must be members of British Dressage and comply with their requirements, as well as those of the British Equestrian Federation, in order to travel abroad to compete.

There were several people I'd need to have on my side if I was intending to follow up on all these invitations and schedules. Di and Clive had to provide continued training and, at times, another horse.

The programme was run by Ann Cutcliffe. She invited riders to training days and organised and set up the venues. Jane Goldsmith was heading a team of trainers and selectors at this time. In these early days, as I've previously mentioned, competitions were done on borrowed horses. However, if you owned a horse you were obliged to transport it to any competition for another rider to use. These venues could be far and wide – Moreton Morrell in Gloucestershire was a favourite, and Talland was also up that way, in Cirencester. Stoneleigh Park was in Warwickshire, the Unicorn Centre in Middlesbrough, and Stow-on-the-Wold also in Gloucestershire, to name but a few.

Then, in 2000, I was delighted to be placed second in the Strongid-P RDA Championships. I'd come second only to Julia Tankard, who was considered an excellent competitor and was also a Paralympian.

Though we had been missed for the Sydney Olympics, we were being encouraged to keep training for Athens in 2004.

The last big event of the season was the SSA National Dressage Championships. We came home from these with a trophy for both the kur and best music, along with several rosettes.

My next goal was to compete at a medium level of dressage, so with the onset of winter it was back to work in earnest. Poor Barbarella and I spent many hours in the freezing school trying to cope with lateral work, flying changes and collection – not the easiest of tasks for a twenty-year-old horse. Di had introduced us to Lizzie Murray, whose mother is Jenny Lauriston-Clarke – one of the country's finest trainers and also an international judge. My local trainer became Claire Evans. At the time she was national champion at medium level and also a fine instructor. Under her guidance we began to make progress.

By the spring I felt that we were ready to try out our new-found skills, but our hopes were dashed by the onset of a nationwide foot-and-mouth epidemic. This was a shattering blow – all competitions were cancelled, and by the time the restrictions were eased in May we had to concentrate only on the events in which we could hope for a high chance of success. We were eagerly looking forward to that year's trials for the RDA international squad, but – of all the maddening things to happen – Bill and I both went down with flu two days before and we were unable to attend.

The first big event in 2001 was the qualifier for the Strongid-P trophy. We came in second, which ensured qualification for the final. We did well enough, but I was a little disappointed that we didn't win – we missed out on first place by one mark! If we'd been able to have a proper ride-in we might have done better.

The following week we were once again off to France. This time seven of the best side-saddle riders from England were in attendance; we made quite a cavalcade! In spite of being 'paraplegic', as I was described over the public announcement system, Barbarella and I kept our end up and again we won the concours and dressage classes. I also led a somewhat ragtag quadrille team. We came in second, despite only having worked the whole thing out in the hour before entering the arena.

To my complete surprise, I was paid the great honour of being awarded a special medal by Christian Martin, the *député* of Maine-et-Loire. The other British riders did very well too, and we all returned home satisfied with our efforts.

I was most unfortunate to miss nearly all of the training sessions for the international squad selection; it was just bad luck that these clashed with the other event. Feeling very guilty about this, even though Ann Cutcliffe had been very understanding, I was delighted to be invited to attend a special session with Jane Goldsmith at South Bucks. I don't know whether or not she was impressed with my performance, but I hope so!

The new venue for the SSA nationals was at Keysoe Equestrian Centre, near Bradford. We arrived at the centre during a very wet and windy day. Despite the weather we managed to splash around quite successfully, finishing up with an impressive trophy for the highest number of points won during the event. I also won the historical-costume class dressed as Queen Marguerite of Spain, just beating Claire Lewis, who rode magnificently on an 'off' side-saddle as the Austrian Princess Margaret.

Barbarella was getting quite used to this sort of thing by now – to the judges' and everyone else's alarm she managed a lap of honour at a canter while almost completely covered by a skirt made from twelve metres of fifty-four-inch-wide fabric.

At Keysoe we met a very disabled lady called Helen, who, because of hip problems, like me, was unable to ride astride. I consider it my duty and pleasure to demonstrate the advantages of side-saddle riding for certain types of disability. Luckily my side-saddle fitted her, so we put her on Barbarella and sent her off to have a go. She came back full of enthusiasm and I gave her a list of my contacts from the north of England who could help get her started. Hopefully we'd see more side-saddle riders at RDA events before long.

The next week we were off to the Strongid-P finals, for the first time competing at medium level. These were being held at Stoneleigh, in Warwickshire. The venue is quite testing as there are several dressage arenas side by side, each with its own set of judges seated in cars, and usually three judges to each arena. This can make for a very busy and noisy environment. I got the call from Bill and Jane that they were ready for me to begin, so I rode around the outside of my allotted arena waiting for the judges to ring the bell or blow a horn, whatever the case might be, to let me know I should enter and commence my routine. It seemed to be an unusually long waiting time, so I asked some spectators if they had heard the judges' horn blow. They indicated that they had, so, being quite unsure of myself, I entered the arena and did my test. As I came out someone told me that one of the judges had tried to catch my eye to hurry me in. From the time when the judges ring their bell or blow their horn there are just forty-five seconds to get into the arena. I was late! I was very worried and confused. This was my first indication that I was developing moderate hearing loss – I hadn't been able to hear the horn. Afterwards one of the judges, who was a very experienced list-one judge, came and told me personally that I had been disqualified for being late. What a pity, as I had the best score! This was just one more problem that I had to live with, but now we knew to prepare each time before competing. In future events, when I was due to have a test called I would listen through a microphoned earpiece and judges were forewarned of my condition before I entered the arena.

I tried to keep up my affiliated dressage competitions as often as they came, but now it was back to work for the winter.

This season we decided to do the pas seul and pas de deux competitions. Bill and I offered to sponsor them. This involved hiring the venue, providing the trophies and other prizes, and also paying for the judges. At South Bucks there was another super little dun horse called Mr Custard. I propositioned Clive to pair him up with Barbarella and me to do a pas de deux at these championships. He agreed and we decided on *The King and I* as our theme music. That meant a suitable costume for each of us: an elaborate dress for me and for Clive to add some flamboyant touches to his. We managed to arrange some practice sessions for our choreography and music, and on the day we were placed second against some pretty strong competition. What fun!

Barbarella's partnership had served me well for two long seasons and we began to wonder how long she'd be able to keep up this level of performance – she was twenty-one, after all. I never imagined that she would manage another two years at this outstanding level of accuracy and energy. We came to depend on Murray, a performance-specialist vet, to keep her fit and able to carry on working happily. However, in order to keep her functioning at her maximum potential the vet bills became quite considerable.

Barbarella and I did four whole seasons together. She did the French nationals three times and the Dutch ones twice. Each year we would begin by qualifying for the RDA and SSA nationals. Then we completed the events which qualified us to be in the national RDA squad, where we competed in Strongid-P and international friendlies. We took part in the SSA's National Dressage Festival and pas seul and pas de deux competitions each year. We were also invited to special festivals that were held at Sotheby's Summers Place Country Estate near Billingshurst, Cowdray, Polo Week, and Highclere Castle's Festival of the Horse. These were all great showpieces for the SSA.

There were also a number of country shows put on by the SSA in the south of England, and I continued to compete in affiliated dressage competitions. This all made for a very busy season each year.

It was our last visit to France that really seemed to take its toll on Barbarella, as we were competing in temperatures of up to 40°C. I can remember doing a kur in a wonderful costume that had several layers of thick silk which completely enveloped her. Poor darling, I have a photo of her performing perfectly, getting a straight 10 for her ten-metre circle and canter, etc. We were dressed up in this heavy costume for some considerable time, before and after the class. In the picture, reproduced on page 63, you can clearly see her tongue hanging out, and it really isn't any wonder! In spite of all these difficulties, and her advancing years, she would always do her very best.

Finally, the day came when I could tell that Barbarella really wasn't up to it any more and I rang Di Redfern to ask her advice. Di and Clive were very willing to have her at South Bucks. She would make a perfect schoolmistress for riders to get their confidence on and to learn the advanced skills that she could teach them. I could still see her from time to time, and, quite unbelievably, she lived well into her thirties.

Bill described her as the ultimate professional: she did exactly what she was paid to do! What a star, and what a remarkable little horse that I was so lucky to know!

CHAPTER THIRTEEN

Enter Martina

Winter had rolled around once more. With Barbarella safely delivered to South Bucks to continue her life as a schoolmistress, the race was on again to find a replacement. I wanted a horse that I could train up to a more advanced level so I could continue furthering my career the next season. *Horse and Hound* magazine would be scoured for any horses for sale, each and every week, as well as any other magazines, contacts and livery yards, all in a frantic effort to find a suitable mount again. We made many phone calls and drove many miles, all with disappointing results. These journeys would take us into some nice places that kept horses and equally some not-so-nice ones. Very often the horse would be out in a field and if I wanted to try it then that's where I rode. I always took a couple of side-saddles with me and, if I wanted to try one out, its owner would have to fit them for me. I never came across a horse that gave any trouble when being fitted with a side-saddle, provided it was a reasonable fit and didn't hurt.

Bill and I visited a very nice yard where we met a beautiful 18-hand dun called Kevin. Bill was rather taken with this gentle giant, but sadly he was not for sale.

Over the course of several weeks and a great deal of mileage we saw at least twenty horses. I was just beginning to worry that this season would be a no-show when Bill found an advertisement that looked promising. We went along to see the mare, taking Claire Evans, my trainer at the time, with us for support and her expert advice. Martina was a chestnut 16.2-hand Swedish warm-blood and only twelve years old. She was owned by a young lady who wanted a 'jumper', and apparently Martina hadn't taken to jumping.

Our first impression was that she was 'very chestnut', but pretty and keen to be friendly. The young lady rode her, but seemed to have no idea of how to show Martina at her best. Claire was itching to get on and had her going beautifully in no time.

It was immediately apparent that it wouldn't be wise to put my side-saddle on this horse's back. Clearly, it wasn't a good enough fit. However, we all liked what we saw and Martina's owner was kind enough to let us borrow her for a week's trial. This was arranged and, with Claire's supervision, I rode Martina cross-saddle and found I liked her a lot. The price was manageable too. Murray, our vet, was called to come and give an examination. He put her through all the tests and paces, as well as getting a detailed history from Martina's owner. Murray knew all the right questions to ask, especially about the horse's temperament.

Eventually, on his recommendation, Martina was bought and delivered to a new livery we had chosen called School Farm at Lockerley, near Romsey in Hampshire. The yard had been purchased as a place for Annie McDonald-Hall to keep her Grand Prix horses. At this time, Annie was among the top ten Grand Prix riders and was still competing. School Farm took me on and bent over backwards to be helpful. I was able to park my car right next to Martina's stable so that I could be involved with her daily care and schooling.

We urgently needed to get my side-saddle fitted to Martina correctly, but Michael Huline-Dickens, the expert, was still in Portugal, where he spent the winter, and wouldn't be back until the spring. In the meantime, Claire was schooling her and I was hacking out quietly with my cross-saddle. We tried a couple of other saddlers to get my side-saddle satisfactorily fitted on Martina, without any success. Time was flying by, but it wasn't long before Michael returned and, true to form, he came and fixed it. There would only be a brief window before the RDA regionals to get Martina up to a good level of performance on side-saddle.

Claire had done some great work on her, which was very helpful as I needed to compete at medium level for my grade-III test and do a freestyle kur at that level as well. In fact, we found that Martina was proving herself to be quite talented. She was not only a quick learner, but she also had good balance, was willingly forward-going and had good connection between her front and hindquarters. Claire actually had her doing some two-time flying changes. She had a natural ability with flying changes at the canter, but at times got a little tense in the back at a medium trot. Even so, what a joy it was to work with her. There was only one downside with Martina – she was terrified of clippers and very nervous about having anything going on around her head and face.

This would be frustrating and time-consuming in a competition horse as there was always a lot of grooming and plaiting up to be done, often under pressure. She obviously needed some help to cope better with this foible of hers. Fortunately, I saw an article in a riding magazine entitled 'We Find Equine Perfection in Seven Oaks'. I was informed that 'Kate Penn and Alan Meyer of Equine Perfection are two of only twenty-seven John Lyons select trainers in Europe.' John Lyons founded and established conditional-response methodology, based on respect and trust control, where willing performance is gained without fear or pain. This could be the answer to a maiden's prayer: hopefully they could help Martina. Before long we were on our way to spend a week or more – whatever it took – at their establishment. Their yard was sparklingly new and first class. Martina quickly made herself at home there and I stayed with my sister-in-law, Pat, who lived about twenty minutes' drive away from the facility.

I took to Kate and Alan instantly. Kate was a fellow Aussie and well travelled. She was also an experienced dressage rider and trainer. Alan had been part of the Sheriff's Mounted Division in Canada and had spent a lot of time training both horses and riders. Their philosophy followed three simple rules during any lesson:

- The horse can't get hurt.
- We can't get hurt.
- The horse must end the lesson calmer than when it started.

I arrived early in the morning for our first day and ensured Martina was ready to begin her regime. I tacked up cross-saddle and Kate rode her. Everything looked very good. The outdoor manége was huge – at least two full-sized dressage arenas – with lovely country scenery all around. The next session was taken by Alan and he got to work on desensitising her fears and phobias through a form of re-education. What patience he had! Martina's insecurities were very deeply ingrained and it seemed that it would take a long while for him to get through to her.

In the afternoon it was my turn to ride her and they were quite interested in my method of riding side-saddle. It was still early days, but we needed to improve in two main areas: transitions, especially trot to canter and vice-versa, and attaining more balance in our half-passes. Martina had to adjust to a stick, and not a leg, to give the aids on the right side. Day after day the focus was not only to make things better, but to have fun and enjoy learning new and different ways of doing things. Martina also had to learn to be more trusting; at first she found this to be difficult, but we soon began to see how Alan was making progress in unlocking her neurotic tendencies. The question was could we maintain this when other people were around? That was to be the real test.

All too soon the week came to an end and an evaluation was done. Both Kate and I agreed that Martina and I had improved our performance skills, but, in spite of his amazing patience and clever techniques, Alan had not been able to solve her intense fear of clippers. Even under mild sedation, she would wake up the minute she heard the sound of them!

Back at School Farm, I was thrilled to discover that Annie was willing to take us on and coach us from time to time. We were able to do a couple of local side-saddle shows and Martina had no trouble with any of my costumes, no matter how much they flapped around her. She also enjoyed the music that Bill had arranged. This was all excellent preparation for the RDA competitions coming up. By now, both Jane and Wendy were getting quite accustomed to her tricky behaviour; in fact they were brilliant at managing her anxiety and ensured she was ready in good time for me to warm up.

We were successful in the regionals at South Bucks, qualifying for grades III and IV. I could only do one class, so I chose to focus on grade III. Our marks were improving into the 60% range and we received several encouraging comments from the judges. We still had six to eight weeks to prepare for the nationals. At Hartpury I was invited to compete in an international friendly on the Friday, but I competed on another horse.

The following Sunday we did our grade-III test and a freestyle kur for the nationals. In the grade test, which was ridden in the outdoor arena, I was delighted to receive a score of 74! We got a 7 for impulsion and a 6 for submission; clearly the judges could see that she was still showing some tension.

Our kur was to be performed in the indoor arena and, as I rode around the outside waiting for the judge to ring the bell, Martina, true to chestnut-mare form, had a great spook at something, knocking the dressage boards flying and generally making a nuisance of herself. Nevertheless, and quite unbelievably, we won the class with a score of 78% and 8s for all our collectives.

The SSA nationals were in less than three weeks' time and our amazing success in the tests ensured we had qualified, but then tragedy destroyed all our hopes. One morning, Sarah, the manager at School Farm, phoned with some terrible news – Martina had put her front leg through a gate and injured herself quite badly. The vet was on her way. School Farm at Lockerley was a round trip of seventy-three miles from Portsmouth, so I wasn't going to be able to get there for at least an hour.

The vet was evaluating Martina's injuries upon my arrival. "Serious" was her initial comment. Martina had cut the tendons under her left pastern. My guess is that she had been flirting with her friend in the next field and had thrown her front leg through the gate. However, this should have been lined with netting to prevent such an accident from happening! We needed to get her to Liphook Equine Hospital, urgently. Roger, my new transporter, was contacted. Yes, he would be able to drop everything on his farm and be there within an hour.

At Liphook, she was seen almost immediately by a surgeon specialising in tendons. The news was grim – Martina had seriously injured herself, slicing through tendons and tendon sheaths. She needed surgery and the prognosis was not good. Even if the operation was a success she would require one and a half years of box rest. This was not the sort of news I wanted to hear. Roger, an experienced breeder of Welsh ponies, was very supportive and understanding. By now he knew enough about Martina to understand how terrible this news was. The surgery was fairly straightforward, though there was no certainty as to the long-term outcome. My mind was spinning and I had to make some very difficult decisions quickly. Martina's issues with scissors and clippers were not her only problems – even farriers and dentists had to treat her with great gentleness and patience. She also didn't like being in her box for any length of time: overnight to sleep was about her limit. We knew that she didn't sedate well either. The thought of having to nurse her for months in her stable filled me with horror. This was quickly turning into a nightmare.

The vet was most helpful in explaining the seriousness of the situation and what my options were, such was her insight into the long-term matter that I was trying to grapple with. She couldn't offer any consolation or positive answers about how to manage the nursing care. My gut feeling was that Martina would not be a good patient and the harrowing memories of Hannah's experience were still fresh in my mind. I was given some time to sit with Martina; her leg was bandaged up, and she was able to munch on some grass. I rehearsed all my options, putting all the pros and cons to Roger. He was most understanding, but the decision had to be mine. Even Bill could not give me a satisfactory answer to my plea, "What should we do?" It's a fact of life when owning a horse that sometimes you need to make tough decisions. I made up my mind and enquired about having her put down. It seemed the best thing to do for Martina's sake. I was there with her at the end. She went down with dignity, unforced, rested, and with no pain. Unfortunately for us, my entire focus had been on the horse's suffering and I'd neglected to approach my insurer before having her euthanised. I was therefore unable to make any claim for her accident.

This was the most talented horse that I'd had, and I was devastated. It was all over, just four days before my SSA nationals. Bill had put some lovely music together that suited her paces and I had a magnificent historical costume for her to carry off. Now, in no time at all, I needed to borrow a horse if I was going to compete. Dear Claire thought that she might have a solution. She was schooling a lovely horse at the time. With the permission of the owner, perhaps I could take him? I hotfooted it to her place to try him out. The most prominent thought in my mind was would my side-saddle fit? Miraculously, the side-saddle sat fairly well on him and he didn't seem to mind it. He was also good-looking and with paces to die for. I was getting excited.

We took him out to Addington so I could try him out and I was delighted to find him very well behaved. The next morning was the first day of the competition and the girls turned him out beautifully. All seemed well in the warm-up for my dressage test and all went to plan when I did the full test in the outdoor arena.

In the afternoon I was to do my musical freestyle in the indoor International Arena. Again we warmed up outside with no problems, but as we entered the indoor arena I could feel him tensing up. I told myself to just relax, keep calm and everything would settle down once we were into the swing of things. My hand went up to indicate that the music should begin and my entry was fine: all the trot work seemed to be together and we seemed to float. The walk was just about all right, but it's not always easy to tell. Looking back, perhaps the tension was beginning to be a real concern. When I asked him to lift into a canter, on the change of music, there was no response. I quickly gave the aid again, but this time he went up into 'airs above the ground'. Normally in a side-saddle one could be reasonably safe to hang on by the emergency grip, but the horse's front feet were just inches from a window and I couldn't understand what this behaviour was all about. I quickly resigned to the fact that I just had to let go, and luckily I had a fairly soft surface to land on. As I fell there was a loud "OH!" from the considerable audience, but within seconds I was surrounded by Bill, the girls and several good friends. Fortunately the only thing hurt was my pride, and I was quickly brushed down and put into my wheelchair.

Meanwhile, His Nibs was taken back to his stable in disgrace. We rang Claire and eventually learnt from his owner that he had previously been a jumper. As is often the case, he didn't take to it and was probably mistreated in the effort. This had given him a phobia about performing at an indoor school. Well, that was that day over with. The next day I would have my costume class. If I couldn't find a horse to wear it on I would just have to go in the ring in my wheelchair.

Bill and Rebekah frantically tried all the friends they knew to find a replacement. At the eleventh hour, Henry was brought around to see me. Now, Henry was a gentle giant and a wonderful schoolmaster. He was owned by Roger Philpot, who, as I've previously mentioned, is one of the SSA's best trainers and ambassadors. Henry had done his day's work already – or so he thought, having given a successful performance with an overseas rider. He was adamant that he'd done enough for the day and wasn't going to give any more. He eventually submitted to be dressed and the girls got to work decking him out in all the regalia. It didn't quite fit in one or two places, but looked passable as long as it wasn't pointed out.

The girls got me mounted with some difficulty; Henry was tall, and my Scottish regimental uniform was complicated by a very long skirt and shawl. I usually mounted from a ladder and it took three or four experienced people to help me up. Jane held the horse still while Rebekah tried to organise the skirt of the costume, often getting lost in the masses of fabric. Bill's job was to aid my legs and feet up on to each rung of the ladder, and finally to the top. Once I reached the summit I was assisted in getting my leg over so I could pull myself into the saddle. Then, with Wendy on one side and Rebekah on the other, my skirts and other sections of the costume were arranged to look exactly like the portrait I was recreating.

With not a minute to spare we entered the arena. "Come on, Henry! Be a bit more enthusiastic and show us both off!" Slow or dead slow seemed to be his only speeds.

The audience could read his thoughts too, and I could hear some whispering: "He's on strike" and "He needs to be paid more for overtime." Fortunately, this class was judged 'at the walk', but it was a large ensemble and the competition was fierce. I was becoming nervous that we weren't doing enough to be noticed and I was acutely aware that the young judge knew her stuff. She was the seamstress who made all the historical costumes for Hampton Court, and we had already won the class several times before. Around we went and I could feel the tension rising. Had we portrayed the Duchess of Gordon in her fine 'Chief of the Gordon Highlanders' uniform to a high enough standard? Henry was still taking it all in his own slow stride and everyone was quite bemused by his attitude. Then, success! We were called in first place! The applause from the audience confirmed the judges' decision. What a roller-coaster ride this had been and now such a marvellous relief and reward. Could Henry now do a lap of honour? Not to worry – the photographer from *Horse and Hound* was waiting patiently to get some beautiful shots of us for the magazine. Afterwards he wanted to know all the correct details of the costume.

At this year's nationals I'd borrowed and ridden four different horses for various classes, but in the end it was Henry that had proved himself to be the perfect pro.

CHAPTER FOURTEEN

Star's Story

It was August, the National SSA Show was over and there were still our regular events and competitions to look forward to before Christmas and the New Year. School Farm was gracious enough to reserve my stable, and we were hoping to find another horse to keep on riding. By now this had become a way of life and, despite my disability, I felt it had really helped me to achieve my maximum potential. My husband, Bill, was still encouraging me to find another horse, but funds were not so plentiful this time round.

We went through the usual procedure of poring over the advertisements in all the equestrian magazines. Once again, there were many phone calls and miles of motoring to be done. We decided to try a dealer, quite far out of our way, near the border with Kent. His business was done from a backyard and he had a dozen stables, full of ponies of all sizes, some of which were quite easy on the eye. We didn't find anything suitable among the stabled animals, but he said he also owned two fields which were full of horses. He was sure that we would find one which would suit me. We drove out to the first field, which was only five minutes away. There were about eight horses in this one and what a motley crew they were! It wasn't just the horses that were unappealing; the field was bare of grass and days of untended dung lay strewn around. A bale of hay had been thrown in for the horses to pick at, but they were also walking it into the mud and peeing on it. It was a not a pretty sight.

Under my breath, I said to Bill, "There's nothing here – let's go!"

My husband is the first to admit he knows nothing about horses and generally keeps well away. However, he has in many instances been my best judge as he has a very humane way of seeing animals.

There was a particularly unfortunate-looking horse among the herd which caught Bill's eye and, seeming to return his attentions, the animal began to make his presence known. Although he was thought to be the runt of the herd, his ears went back and he fiercely sent the rest of the group packing. Bill went over to him and the creature seemed to be friendly and agreeable. This was not what I wanted to happen, but 'animals choose you', as they say. They are very intuitive, sensitive and insightful. If they set their minds to it, they know exactly how to wrap you around the proverbial hoof or paw. The inquisitive herd began to come in for a closer look, but once again he chased them away – he really did want us to notice him. Of course, the dealer was quick to pick up on this and offer me a ride. Though I'd done it many times before, dear me, I was not about to engage in the rigmarole of putting a side-saddle on a back that had no padding and then riding this strange horse around his decrepit field. I managed to persuade Bill to take me to lunch. There I hoped to convince him of the folly he was getting us into.

For some reason this horse still played on Bill's mind – and also on mine, but for a totally different reason. Somehow I was persuaded into going back to have a second look.

The dealer, though surprised to see us again, went through his usual spiel and I, against my better judgement and with Bill's assistance, managed to get myself and my side-saddle mounted on the horse. By this point we had learnt that his name was Star; he was around twelve years old, 16.2-hands and an ex-national hunter. He was dark bay with a white star on his forehead; I guessed that was his namesake.

I was desperate to dismount, get out and put the whole experience behind me. We had plenty of other stables on our list to visit that day. Bill, I have learnt over the years of being married to him, has a charitable heart when he sees an animal in need of rescue. We have had several cats, all of which we adopted from RSPCA centres and showered with love and affection for the rest of their happy little lives. I was getting anxious that he was convinced that Star needed just that – rescuing, and someone who would improve his life.

"If anyone can make something of this horse's life, you can" was Bill's plea. As I turned my back on the scene and began to make my way out, Bill stopped me and in a sorrowful voice continued: "I can't have that horse's life on my mind if we don't take him." Star would have gone for cat's food at a fraction of the asking price.

This was a battle that I couldn't fight any more; it was completely out of my control. There was no need to call a vet to check his vitals, just to get him delivered to School Farm. Roger even had to go and fetch him.

On arrival Star almost fell out of the lorry, such was his poor condition. Sarah, the manager, was shocked to see the appearance of such an animal. She was used to seeing only top-quality horses in her yard. Nevertheless, she and her staff were wonderful. Star seemed to win the hearts of everyone he met. He was lovable, friendly and a complete clown. With Sarah's feed regimen, time out in a good field, and other friendly horses and people around, Star blossomed. After a while we called in Murray to check Star over. He gave him a good bill of health and remarked that he seemed younger than his years suggested.

It was five or six weeks before I could contact Michael to come and adjust my side-saddle and finally begin to ride Star.

Claire took him over to her yard for a week to give him some expert schooling, and I only rode him after she had warmed him up.

By now he was filling out everywhere; no ribs could be seen, and his neck, shoulders and limbs were rounded and muscling up in all the right places.

Soon after this I spent a week with Star at Jenny Lauriston-Clarke's farm, where Lizzie Murray took us in hand. Lizzie also rode him side-saddle, beautifully, which gave us an edge on his progress. Star's natural way of going seemed 'long and low'; and although he wasn't happy about it, we tried to get him to collect more. He appeared to have some thoroughbred behavioural tendencies and couldn't get his head around the multitude of transitions we were asking of him. I decided that, once again, Kate and Alan might be able to assist. We went over to Seven Oaks to spend another week indulging in their expert care.

They both put a lot of time into trying to teach him to focus and to accept that the rider was in charge and expected more from him. During one session, Kate was trying to collect him so he would use his hindquarters more, and he seemed to be getting the hang of a few piaffe steps, when suddenly he decided that he'd had enough and just took off – fortunately after Kate had dismounted, but with reins hanging and stirrups dangling. Well! Did he go! We were dumbfounded and stood aghast while he galloped around the arena in a turmoil. He was like a pressure cooker letting off all its steam at once. All three of us decided that we would have to back off for a while and maybe give him another year before we tried to develop his skills further.

We spent the winter working hard in preparation for the season in spring. There were several SSA area shows and then the RDA regionals. Once again, we qualified with percentages only in the low 60s, but in spite of this we went to Hartpury for the nationals. We didn't disgrace ourselves – in fact it was one of the most successful RDA nationals that I'd had the good fortune to attend. I hoped to do as well, if not better, at the SSA nationals in just a few weeks' time.

By now Star was looking really very handsome. He'd filled out and muscled up and had a lovely gleaming coat. He was showing himself to be quite the joker, always wanting to be noticed, and I was not allowed to talk to anyone without including him. If he felt left out he would pick something up and throw it – often one or both of my walking sticks, which I usually hung over his stable door. He had another clever act which he would do with my sticks – I called it his 'Fred Astaire'. He would pick them up and appear to do a juggling routine, in a playful manner, before once again throwing them in our general direction to get attention. I frequently had to wash and polish them after he'd finished toying with them, and in the end just kept a pair exclusively for his games.

Bill usually steered clear of getting familiar with any of my other horses, but he had a real soft spot for Star. I think it had been love at first sight for both of them.

Once again, Bill was busy putting music together for various tests and freestyles. We were going to attempt both the novice and elementary-level freestyles, as well as several other showing classes to music and in costume.

As before, I'd made a truly wonderful historical costume. I went to a lot of trouble to ensure the various bits and pieces of apparel fitted Star perfectly. There were lots of practice tests and, when anything went wrong or didn't go as planned, Bill would always adamantly defend Star's performance. Quite sweet, really!

The SSA nationals were at Addington this year and during the first morning's event Star seemed to take the dressage tests in his stride. In the afternoon we had our big costume class and, after a number of years' experience, the girls Jane and Wendy were quite the experts in preparing Star in all his complicated regalia. My costume portrayed the wedding outfit worn by Henrietta Maria, the sixteen-year-old French wife of King Charles I, and as usual Rebekah was on hand to assist me in dressing. The costume was elaborate in every way and included an intricate bridle, hanging breast piece, and a massive throw-over rug which completely covered Star's back and hung just inches from the ground. There was never enough time for a dress rehearsal, but the team were usually brilliant at getting it right on the day. Star seemed ten feet tall and enjoyed immensely the attention lavished on him as we entered the arena.

The judge's comment was "This is the costume to beat all costumes!"

Star had done us proud and I'd racked up another costume win.

We were not so fortunate in the costume concours d'élégance, a class where one would wear period costumes which did not have to maintain the strict level of authenticity seen in the historical class. Our pretty take on Alfred de Dreux's *An Elegant Equestrian* portrait did not go down well. In fact, the judge said that the colour of the saddle cloth 'offended the eyes'! Well, I've learnt that you can't always please a judge's eyes.

Pairs are always fun and this year I teamed up with my friend Becky Taylor, who had recently acquired a lovely bay horse – he would make a super match for Star. Becky and I had paired up in previous years, when I was riding Barbarella and she was on a pretty dun called Charlie. Becky had ridden Charlie the previous year and had won the prize for best junior rider at the nationals, but this year we both had new horses. The competition was just as strong as ever, with about eight pairs in the class. We did a circuit of the arena before commencing with our little show. Both our horses seemed very happy working together. Clever Becky rode in her 'off' side-saddle which meant that she was on my right. This symmetry looked very elegant, but we both had to be careful with our sticks so as not to give each other's horses a jab. A beautiful grey pair won the class, though we were very happy to come in second place and join in the lap of honour at the end. All in all, this had been a very successful nationals and Star had proven himself to be a real star.

Back at School Farm, there was still plenty of work to be done to bring Star up to the next stage of his schooling. His fitness levels had improved immensely, and once or twice during his training he would take off at a gallop with me in tow. Fortunately we were in the indoor school so he wasn't able to do any damage to either of us. This was yet another warning that he couldn't cope mentally with the pressure and accuracy I was demanding of him and to which he should by now be accustomed. One day, as we were hacking out around the vast School Farm fields, a young white-tailed deer only a few yards from us was disturbed by our presence and ran into the undergrowth. Star immediately sprang around and literally catapulted me out of the saddle.

This was an overreaction, I thought. Fortunately I wasn't hurt and hung on to the reins so he didn't run off. However, there was the small matter of me either getting back on to a 16.2-hand horse or of walking the fair distance back to the stables. Neither seemed a realistic option! The answer to my prayers was not long in coming. Another livery friend came into view and I hailed her. Fortunately, she could see what had happened and went for the right help.

I was now having serious doubts about Star's suitability for the job. It was around this time that I fell ill again and was not able to keep up with the exercise programme that he required. It was suggested that we give him to a young lady to look after; she had a large field and kept several other horses there. I kept in touch by phone and was always reassured that Star was fine and being looked after. Sadly, when I recovered enough to go and see him he was in a poor state. Not only had he been turned out in boots which had rubbed his fetlocks raw, but he had on a head collar that had scraped a bloody area on his cheeks, and his rug had been left on without any regular checks of his coat. I rang Jane Davies, who had a yard called Brantwood Orchard. She was not far away in Curdridge, Hampshire. Jane was very understanding about Star's whole story, the mishaps and that above all he needed a more suitable life than the one I wanted him for. Jane had the answers to my problem. She took Star in, got him on track again and ensured he was less 'fizzed up'. Within a few weeks she had a good home lined up for him to go to.

A family bought him – the father wanted to ride, the son wanted a horse and the whole family fell in love with him. I received a lovely letter from them, thanking me for training Star so well and saying that he was just what they dreamed of finding in a horse. This was about ten years ago, but I rang Jane again recently. She remembered Star and me – she is still in business, finding the right horses for the right people. How nice is that! There are people like Jane out there who think of a creature's welfare first and have the skills and passion to match up the right animal to the right home and owners.

By now I'd had about ten years' riding experience and there was so much more that I wanted to develop and achieve. Riding doesn't change your disability, but it helps you to learn new and different ways of dealing with it. It helped me to perform at my maximum rather than my minimum. In the early days my legs used to go into terrible spasms when riding cross-saddle, but learning to ride side-saddle had helped me to avoid this discomfort and still feel safe. All this travel and competing had given me so much confidence that I'd come to believe that no dream was beyond my reach – with the right help, of course! I was aware of the classical equitation method of riding and training the horse from my earliest days as a disabled rider. I joined the Classical Riding Club (CRC) in 1997, and began reading the teachings of the old masters of dressage Alois Podhajsky and Henry Wynmalen. I had visited the Spanish Riding School, as it is called, in Vienna twice before I'd become disabled, and I had also been made aware of the work of Sylvia Loch in the UK. I made sure I had one of her books on my library shelf! I was lucky enough to pick a livery where Claire Lilley taught and kept her horses. She was schooling her young Andalusian, Amadeus, at the time. She had spent some time in Germany and trained under Herr Hans Heinrich Meyer zu Strohen, so she really knew her horses. Around the same time I become a member of the TTT (Training the Teachers of Tomorrow), a charity based at East Whipley Farm, Shamley Green. There, we attended classes and teach-ins by senior instructors such as Steven Clarke. Several times a year, I also attended international clinics by Arthur Kottas-Heldenberg of Vienna. I competed in several CRC dressage competitions at medium level, though their test sheets and scores are a little different from affiliated British Dressage. Leading on from this, I was often fortunate to engage with other trainers who understood this level of instruction. Thus, my own skills and understanding of training a horse in the correct way were improving greatly. What I needed now was a horse that had the breeding, conformation and willingness to learn at an advanced level.

I was always relieved and thrilled when a trainer took on board, without any hesitation, my methods of equine schooling, even though they hadn't trained that way themselves. The rules are still the same, as I have often said to BD judges when I rode a test this way. In fact, it was found that my understanding of balance and independent seat was exceptionally good. It wasn't always easy to transfer all this knowledge through to the horse one was riding at the time, but it was the theory that the horse should be willing and able to go forward, in self-carriage and in a balanced and elegant manner in all three paces – walk, trot and canter. In choosing a horse one had to consider some important criteria. I was not young, and quite seriously disabled, so my safety was paramount. Therefore the age of the horse usually had to be considered and a good temperament was essential. Then one looked for trainability, experience, track record (if any) and – the big one – price.

CHAPTER FIFTEEN

Lucky

The search for the perfect horse was on, yet again. I was not getting any younger and the years were passing by all too quickly. Time was not on my side – not a good situation to be in when looking for a special kind of mount. Once again, my husband was both encouraging and supportive. Without him I could never have achieved all that I'd done so far, and I accepted that he should have the final word on any decisions that we made.

Many friends were keeping their eyes out for a suitable horse – one whose back would fit my side-saddle. Some weeks went by with no success. One day, in a *Horse and Hound* magazine, Bill saw an advertisement for a horse that seemed ideal. I phoned the owner of the livery straight away. Bill insisted that we should go and see this one.

On first impressions, it was a well-heeled yard with a good manége. There was a bay mare tied up in the stable block. She was nicely groomed and in a good, well-rounded condition. I walked over to talk to her, quite slowly as I was on my sticks, and as I did she had her gaze on me. She gave a welcoming nicker that was a bit alarming coming so soon. I, however, took it as a delightfully friendly gesture. As I looked her over, taking my time and asking questions of the agent, she still wouldn't take her eyes off me. They were deep, dark and soft, and she oozed kindness and warmth. Oh God, my heart began to beat a bit faster. Lucky was her name, and she had good breeding from old Hanoverian stock. She was 16.2 hands and fifteen years old. What was the story behind this lovely horse? I wondered. Her present owner was a young lady who had owned her for only two or three years, at most. Lucky was on full livery and was trained regularly by the owner of the yard. Her owner had developed a problem with her back and had been advised to give up riding to help her recover. In contrast to this, I find that the time I spend riding gives me the most relief from my aches and pains and know of others who concur.

Lucky was saddled up and ridden for me so that I could see her paces and the way she 'went'. I noticed that the walk was not her best pace, nor the canter, but her trot work was very expressive. Basically, she looked weak in the hindquarters. Her outline was a little long and low, but this improved as she warmed up. I liked what I could see so far. They were asking a price that I didn't think matched up with what I'd seen, though, so I said that we had another horse to look at that day and we would have to think about it.

Meanwhile, I got advice from friends, and Bill and I did some sums. That night I couldn't get Lucky out of my mind. What had she done to make such an impression on me so quickly? We decided to go and have a second look; her livery was in the Farnham area, less than an hour's drive from Portsmouth. This time I would take a couple of side-saddles and a carrot or two. Once again, she was tied up in exactly the same place. As I parked my car and began heading towards her, she gave me a very enthusiastic whinny. As I've said more than once before, animals choose you! However, I had some important things that I wanted to get right this time around and I really didn't want to get emotionally carried away about an animal that wasn't going to be able to deliver the goods.

She was ridden again for me and I could feel myself trying

to look for the best in her performance, though deep down I had some doubts. I had to try her out myself, and that meant that one of my side-saddles would have to fit her well enough for me to be secure enough in my seat to get a feel of her way of going! She was very broad in the shoulders and didn't have a very high wither, which meant that we couldn't get a good fit, but I managed to get on. She walked off – not too bad at the walk, but the minute we went into a little trot the saddle slipped forward up her shoulder. That wasn't good at all and it spooked her a little bit. Nevertheless, I made up my mind that I didn't want to lose this horse, but I needed a second opinion. There were others who were interested in seeing Lucky, so I would either have to take a chance or let her go. Bill began to negotiate what he considered a fair price and also rang the bank manager to see if we could afford her.

Temperament has always been an important priority and Lucky had it all; it was just this weak back end that I had some concerns about. Even then I felt I was just making excuses and was quietly confident that I could improve her performance. We rang Murray, our vet, and he came to check her over. By this time I had known Murray for about ten years and he had been involved with all my horses. He knew very well what my needs were and what I could do to improve a horse's performance. We both noticed that Lucky's front right hoof was a little smaller than the left one. She also had thrush in all four feet, and that was a problem that I had never dealt with before. He rigorously put her through all the tests, including X-rays done with a portable machine, and couldn't find anything specific that would make her fail the vetting. It was just the feet. Even her back showed no lameness, signs of pain or anything else that would put a question mark on her ability.

"Could we treat the feet?" was my next question, and of course we could.

We were now slightly pressured into making a decision

because someone else was wanting to make arrangements to see Lucky. Bill had come to an agreement with the bank manager and was eager for me to make the purchase. I felt experienced enough at this point to be able to make a reasonably sound judgement. I knew I could work with this horse and better her performance. I just hoped I was not mistaken.

Soon, Lucky was delivered to School Farm. The next thing was to get Michael down as soon as possible to fit my side-saddle so that I could get started. The first thing Sarah, the manager, had to deal with was that Lucky was not used to going out into a field alone. In fact, she wasn't too keen to go out at all. I offered to stay with her, for an hour or so at a time, to get her used to her new surroundings. Sarah said that she'd find a little companion for her to go out and stay with.

Over a period of time, and with a lot of patience and perseverance, we learnt how to manage this funny foible. At last I was able to leave her in Sarah's care. My time for riding each day was after lunch. That meant that I was driving down the M27 at the least busy time of the day and returning home before the evening rush. She seemed to be having a good time at the livery – she would go out in the field with her little friend, come in for some hay and lunch, then have a little rest before I arrived. The yard was also fairly quiet and I could use the facilities without having to share them with too many others. Lucky was not concerned about being ridden and schooled side-saddle; nor were any of my helpers and trainers – they were just there to assist me in getting the best out of another mount. By now I'd had Barbarella, Martina and Star at School Farm, and Sarah and Co. had looked after them all. Annie had given me lots of excellent help, and other trainers came there regularly.

I soon learnt that Lucky wasn't an easy ride; she was intelligent and powerful, and I had plenty of horse underneath me. She had a very strong will and wanted to have things her way. There was nothing nasty or dangerous about her way – she just had bags of energy. I talked to Sarah about this and she decided it was necessary to reduce her feed intake. It really didn't take much to get her all fired up – one of my instructors described her as "on a mission!" I now thought I realised why Lucky had had five different novice lady owners in her fifteen-year life. None of them had kept her for more than two or three years. Was this the reason why Lucky latched on to me so urgently and so soon? Did she see something in me that she needed? Who knows? The point now was that I had a horse who needed a very wise, patient yet competent rider to cope with her. Was I up to the job? I needed very experienced trainers now; so my first choice was Michel Assouline, who trained many of the para-riders. We spent a week at his yard to get some intensive training in. One of Michel's first remarks was that "This horse is on a mission," confirming the previous instructor's observation. How interesting, but how could we deal with it? He decided he needed to try Lucky out himself, and from then on he was able to give me some useful and sensible tips. She needed lots of leg, especially for downward transitions and to help keep her hindquarters underneath her and engaged. To practise this we did lots of canter circles, even ten-metre ones, and we started to piaffe along the wall, using a stick to get her legs underneath. She was very hard work for me, but, as always, I thrived on the challenge. There was something about Lucky which I loved tremendously. She was most expressive; her eyes and ears did the talking while her body language remained quiet and composed. She wanted lots of love and kisses and she endeared herself to everyone. I was beginning to be able to read her like a book.

I was invited to a judge and trainers' workshop day at South Bucks. Following advice given to me by my dressage friends, as well as well-respected members of the SSA, I was now a judge in training. On this particular day, Nicola McGiven gave a very capable display on a horse that she was training. Nicola was on the national British Dressage team and both Di Redfern and I were impressed by her abilities. Nicola's yard was not far from South Bucks and she kindly agreed to Lucky and me spending a week there under her tuition. The spring was fast coming on and we still had quite a bit of preparation to do before we could go out and compete.

Nicola's yard was beautiful. The stables were first class and the indoor school had dressage mirrors, which were ideal for us. Lucky had a tendency to lean on the left rein; perhaps she was overcompensating for a weakness in her right hind leg? Her left canter was not as good as the right, either. Was she guarding against some weakness or problem? We decided to focus on strengthening her back and keeping it relaxed to encourage more collection. The week flew by and we soon found ourselves back home at School Farm. It was now time to decide which tests we would be competing in this season and arrange routines to practise; and, of course, Bill would select music for us to perform to.

Just as in previous years, we needed a few local competitions to get us started and to see how we were going to work together. Judges and their marks differed quite a bit in these early trials. The primary goal is that the two of you – horse and rider – are forming a bond of trust in order to develop a true partnership.

The regional RDA Championships came fairly early in May and we hoped to give an accurate performance at South Bucks. I had a pretty good track record there already, so I knew it was up to Lucky to continue to maintain my high standards. What a good girl she was! We won our class and the nationals at Hartpury were assured. Now we needed a SSA competition where we could try out a costume class and a musical freestyle. Area 8 were holding a national dressage competition at the Arrow Riding Centre in Dartford, Kent. Lorna, Lucky's previous owner, was very keen to follow

Lucky's progress with her new mistress and said that she would film us. A video recording is always an excellent way of checking where one needs to improve as the camera doesn't lie, and it is helpful to see one's mistakes first hand. It is a good teaching and learning tool too.

The SSA classes that suited us were novice and elementary freestyle to music and freestyle to music with costume. It is always a gamble which to choose; all four in one day and maybe you're biting off more than you can chew. On the other hand, if you can manage the times it can be good practice. We entered all classes with just a short break for lunch. My SSA friends were all agog over my new horse. They had been very supportive in the past and were confident that I could still enjoy competing for some time to come. They, too, hoped that I'd found a horse who could live up to my ambitious dreams. Our warm-up class didn't come off so well, but Lucky slowly got into the swing of things. The afternoon, when we got into our costumes and rode to music, went very well. Once again, Bill won the trophy for the best music. The audience also seemed to appreciate my choice of costume. It was a good show all round. Lorna was very impressed with our performance and, as she knew Lucky very well, this gave me a good indication that we were moving in the right direction.

I am fortunate enough to have a set of professional photos from Lucky's first year competing at the Hartpury RDA nationals. Lorna paid us another visit after our grade-III test. As we came out of the arena, she ran up to greet us with a beaming smile and some nice compliments about our performance. "She had a mega trot!" was one of her comments, and we hoped that the judge was of the same mind.

Jane and Wendy were always keen for us to enter the 'turnout' class and I have many trophies as testaments to their hard work. Unfortunately, this time out the judge was not so impressed with us. I knew that the girls were usually flawless in their turnout preparation work, with keen eyes for cleanliness and a great attention to detail. I was sorry for them after all the work that had gone into making us look superb. Lucky had caught many an eye and I thought that she had done me proud. We didn't go home empty-handed either. Among our admirers were Lyn Bennyson and Val Cadman, who ran the Shelley Centre for Therapeutic Riding near Colchester, Essex. They were most interested in side-saddle riding and not only praised what I was doing but wanted to know how to go about it for one of their young riders in particular. After a long conversation it was suggested that Lucky and I pay a visit to the centre and let some of their riders have a go. We were very flattered to find another establishment so interested in side-saddle, and arrangements were made for Lucky and me to visit them at the Shelley Centre. As it was en route to Michel and Metta's yard we could enjoy the best of both worlds – a training session and a day at the Shelley Centre. Roger showed up in his lorry, happy to sleep in it, and Jane also joined us. The centre staff and instructors had made a real occasion of our visit. I was amazed at the number of promising riders who had turned out to see us. Lucky and I gave a short display and talk about how to ride side-saddle, then we opened a 'free for all' invitation for anyone who wished to try it out first-hand.

The SSA nationals were held in August and this year it teemed with rain. Although we were fortunate enough to be in the indoor stable block at Addington, we were nearly flooded out. We had been allocated two stables – one for the horse and one as an office-cum-dressing room. We put tarpaulin on the floor, and curtains on the walls to give us privacy, and there was camping furniture for comfort. We had to share it as a feed room as well, but the bales of hay sometimes came in useful and could double up as tables or additional seats. When the rainwater almost overwhelmed us it was the bales of hay that saved the day. The flood came within inches of our stables and there was considerable sweeping and brushing to get rid of the menacing unwanted water. Fortunately the downpour was sudden, fast and furious and soon passed over, leaving us with better weather for the rest of the show. Mercifully, the water worry was over. I have been in a few similar circumstances when heavy rain has caused me to cancel a costume class because, after a lot of preparation with fabrics that don't take kindly to getting wet, it's just not worth it.

We entered many classes that year – elementary and medium dressage and a freestyle to music, which gave Bill an opportunity to show off his skills. We also took part in the 'mature lady rider' class. This class had a long list of ladies of a certain age and I came in second yet again. In the veteran horses' class – another class with many beautiful entries – Lucky didn't get a look-in, unfortunately. We were not dressed appropriately, and by the time we switched our silk toppers for hard hats we were running a little late. I assume this did not go down too well with the judges!

For a bit of fun, and for the first time at the nationals, we entered into the 'rococo' class, otherwise known as the Ravo Cripps Memorial Pas Seul. This class was sponsored and organised by Jenny Oakley, another good friend to me. There were set movements to be coordinated, but they could be performed in any order. Props and various parts of the costume could be worn by the rider and/or horse, and any article could be discarded during the performance. Costume and music had to tell a story, with drama and acting to make for real entertainment.

I chose a historical theme so that I could wear a beautiful costume based on a Sir Godfrey Kneller portrait from 1715 depicting Frances Pierrepont, the Countess of Mar. It was inspired by events of that year – the Jacobites, led by the Earl of Mar, rebelled against George I's government. The rebellion was initially successful in Scotland, but was soon quashed by the King's forces. The Earl and Countess were forced to flee for their lives, heavily disguised. Safe in Rome, the Countess again dressed in fine clothes and danced for joy to the music of their contemporary J. S. Bach. This class was the speciality of a number of the best side-saddle riders – among them Claire Lewis, who performed brilliantly. Lucky was not on her best form, however. The weather was very hot and, as we discovered afterwards, this had given her a slight sore under her girth. Nevertheless we placed in the top half of the winning places.

Highclere Castle open their extensive and beautiful grounds to a Festival of the Horse each year. The SSA is always invited to give a display in our period and historical costumes. We usually perform right in front of the castle, which gives us a wonderful backdrop. Our very good friends Wes and Elizabeth, from Australia, joined us there and shared our picnic. Elizabeth helped me to get into my costume: Henrietta Maria's wedding dress. Lucky, too, had to wear a considerable amount of regalia and a very deep saddlecloth. This wasn't an easy costume to wear in a class which involved trot and canter. Fortunately the large brimmed hat, which was dripping in ostrich feathers, stayed in place; but unfortunately an earring, which was made of enormous pearl drops and would have been worth a king's ransom originally, somehow managed to detach itself from one of my ears. Maybe someone will find it one day and think it should be at home in a castle? Elizabeth took some fine photos of the pageant. Soon after our friends returned to Australia we learnt that Wes had passed away. We were so very sad, but at least we'd shared some lovely memories.

One day, as I was getting some shopping at the local tack shop, a young lady was introduced to me by Jo, the manageress. Zeb Graham-Howard was her name and she poured her heart out to me. For some time she had been suffering from severe hip pain and had been unable to ride her horses. She wondered whether riding side-saddle would be possible and if I could give her any advice.

"Come and try it out" was my reply. "I have a trustworthy horse who goes side-saddle. When can you come?"

I soon learnt that Zeb was an extraordinary girl – a true animal lover and 'whisperer'. She arrived at School Farm and immediately loved what she saw in Lucky. Likewise, Lucky had an extraordinary reaction to Zeb. It almost seemed as though they spoke the same language. Anyhow, Zeb mounted side-saddle and for the first fifteen minutes or so I helped her to maintain the correct seat and talked her through how to use her left leg and right hand, equipped with a stick, to replace the movement of her right leg. After a few minor seat corrections, she quickly got the hang of it and began to feel free and confident. I suggested that, due to her previous ailments and because this was her first time riding side-saddle, she should only stay on for about fifteen minutes. Everything seemed to have gone very well, but Zeb was reluctant to get off Lucky. I began to grow concerned for her, but my worries were ill-founded. I have never seen someone so ecstatically happy after riding a horse. Certainly Lucky was a very nice horse, but (for the first time?) "No pain!" was the cry and "This is wonderful!"

"Do come again – Lucky won't mind!" was my reply.

The next time Zeb visited us she brought some of her friends who wanted to try side-saddle. Word soon got out that Rayna's horse, Lucky, was a catalyst for ladies who were curious about riding side-saddle. I rather enjoyed seeing others learning a new skill and very much revelling in their experience. I could see myself taking on a slightly different role now; however, I would need to get a teaching qualification and insurance if Lucky and I were going to do this regularly. Sadly, that's how things are now and litigation is on every professional's mind. Due to my disability, my peers at the SSA were very nervous about me taking the instructor's exam. One of the requirements meant that I would have to lunge a horse. Since I couldn't stay on my feet, I couldn't work out a way of doing that while keeping the animal and myself safe. As the people I was trying to teach also had some form of disability, I decided to investigate what was required to go down the RDA route.

Also around this time, I was faced with another challenge regarding Lucky's continued development. Her schooling was not going as easily as I had hoped. Instead of strengthening her hindquarters, I was detecting some reluctance in her ability to carry out flying changes. In the past I had been able to teach elderly horses to develop this skill when others had given up. Barbarella was over twenty years old when she finally 'got it', so I wasn't going to give up on Lucky just yet. Better get Murray to check her over, I decided.

His diagnosis was that she had some inflammation in her suspensory ligaments and he gave her some form of shock wave treatment. Following on from this, it was recommended that we give it time to heal and that I should just walk her for four to six months. This didn't seem like it would be too much of a problem, so I got out my cross-saddle and we began to acquaint ourselves with the local country lanes, streets and even busy roads. This was another learning curve for me, because Lucky seemed to take the lead. Mostly she chose our route, sometimes heading down dead ends and cul-de-sacs. If I said beforehand, "It's no good going down here, love," she would ignore my better judgement and insist on finding out for herself. Nothing fazed her – fortunately, even what one would think of as scary, such as roadworks, etc. Strangely they just made her more curious. She was a joy to be around, and this sense of freedom was wonderful for me as well. I've always said that "With wheels or a horse underneath me I have total freedom and independence."

The weeks and months went by and it seemed that she was getting better in every way. Her walk was relaxed and she used all of her body in every stride. I also wondered if this way of going was helping me in many small and subtle ways. I've learnt in recent years that my polio has also affected my central nervous system. This gives me problems with my balance and focus, and spasms, not just in my legs, but in general. Of course on some days this was more noticeable than others, and some activities were more likely to aggravate my symptoms, but I hoped that the slow pace of these months had helped me physically. I was keen to return to our training.

CHAPTER SIXTEEN

Entertainment at the RDA Nationals

One day I received a phone call from Doug Smith, the chief organiser of the RDA nationals. Doug was also an active instructor and leading light in his own RDA group. To my astonishment, he asked me if I would like to organise the Saturday-evening entertainment at this year's nationals.

"Do you mean a side-saddle evening, Doug?" was my thrilled yet daunted reaction.

"Yes!" was the resounding answer.

'What a wonderful opportunity!' I thought. At the same time I was overwhelmed by the responsibility.

We had only a few months to prepare, so I began by making a long series of phone calls to all of my side-saddle friends and acquaintances. One by one they all confirmed their willingness to take part. They were happy to attend Hartpury and travel from all corners of the country at their own expense – how generous is that? I think that, like myself, they considered this a marvellous opportunity to promote side-saddle, especially for any disabled persons wanting to try this way of riding. By now I had a number of friends coming to School Farm from time to time to ride Lucky. They were all sold on the side-saddle method.

As a matter of courtesy, I had to contact John Mace, chairman of the SSA Area 14, which included Hartpury, to advise him of the invitation and ask for his group's assistance.

John was extremely encouraging and supportive, though he didn't think that any of their riders would be able to contribute to the event.

I was gathering an exciting team of able-bodied and disabled riders with a remarkable variety of talents which I could call upon for the evening's entertainment. I began to make up a programme which included everyone. There were a total of eleven items, all different. Bill had to create music for most of them.

On the day, Bill followed a script which he and I had put together. After the customary introduction of "Ladies and gentlemen, boys and girls" – half the audience was made up of young disabled competitors – we got into the swing of things. "Welcome to this evening of elegance. This will be a different experience than what you're accustomed to as every item in our programme will be ridden side-saddle by ladies from the SSA, as well as a number of disabled riders.

"Entering the arena is a ladies' quadrille – Claire Lewis, Paula Keely, Helen Hogarth and Rayna Matthews. They represent the cream of the SSA world; several have just returned from France, where they competed very successfully against the champions of a number of European nations. They are going to ride to Handel's *Cuckoo and the Nightingale*, the Organ Concerto in F Major."

The quadrille was made up of four well-matched bays, and the ladies wore their formal evening dress of black habit, silk topper and veil, cream silk cravat and gloves. Though we had only had a short time to rehearse beforehand, we were all experienced riders and hoped that we were able to carry it off on the night, as they say.

A few weeks before the nationals I'd been asked to judge a pony-club display. I was mightily impressed by the winner of one of the events. It was a dance routine by Juliet Nunn and her mother, Vanessa. Juliet was a ten-year-old special-needs rider and Vanessa taught dance. I suggested that they try side-saddle, which they took up with enthusiasm, and now here they were at Hartpury giving an impressive display in front of an audience of connoisseurs.

We had enough disabled ladies to make up another quadrille. All of us in this display were wheelchair users, some very disabled. This line-up was made up of Sarah, Amanda, Susannah and myself. Our skills varied, depending on our degree of disability, but we all enjoyed side-saddle. For some of us this was the only way that we could ride. The choreography for this display had to show each rider's ability while ensuring our safety. Sarah, who had absolutely no fear whatsoever, went off into a canter around the other riders. I heard an "Oooh" from the audience at her bravery. To finish, Lucky did a little turn, while the others walked in and out of circles to music by William Boyce.

Tilly Shepherd and her pony, Blue, had visited us at School Farm in the hope that I could help them go side-saddle. Tilly was then ten years old and had difficulties with her lower body and legs. She had first tried side-saddle only a few weeks before the event, but she took to it like a duck to water. So enthused was Tilly by her experience that she managed to find her own side-saddle to fit her pony. She rode, with the help of Imogen, her carer, as an assistant, to an accompaniment of piano arrangements by Felix Mendelssohn and Franz Liszt.

Also assisted by Imogen was Thelma Shepherd, Tilly's twin sister. She had tried out side-saddle on Lucky at the same time as Tilly and she wanted to show what she and Blue had achieved in just a few weeks. Thelma rode to some light music, which included Frédéric Chopin's *Raindrop Prelude*.

There was a short interval, then the microphone was taken over by our good friend Caroline Wilkins – at the time a student at Hartpury. Bill and I had watched her progress since she was a little girl and Caroline was a first-class side-saddle rider. She had also gained experience of microphone use and compèring during her time at college.

Next came a display of beautiful historical costumes. Describing these riders and their costumes really put Caroline to the test, but she managed to get all the details correct. The riders, both adult and junior, were under the firm control of Peta Roberts, herself an instructor at Hartpury College, several times Side-Saddle Rider of the Year, judge, fellow of the British Horse Society (BHS), and much more besides. Along with herself, she led her three young children – Georgie, Bea, and Juliet. All the children and their ponies were in costume. For safety reasons children in costume had to wear a hard hat. That didn't stop them disguising their hard hats in the most brilliant and incredible ways – with wigs, other hats, headdresses and anything else which matched the period of the costume they were featuring in. Then came Elizabeth Rogers, also five times Rider of the Year, with Paula and Helena. Paula was dressed as the Countess of Oxford appeared in 1716. Helena and Elizabeth were dressed as Victorian ladies from the 1850s. They were accompanied by Mozart's *Eine Kleine Nachtmusik*.

As previously mentioned, the SSA has a competitive class called a pas seul. The rider gives a display to music, in appropriate costume, and she acts out a storyline at the same time. Claire Lewis had taken part in the pas seul at the nationals and won on several occasions. She performed to 'Diamonds Are a Girl's Best Friend'. Claire's costume wouldn't have seemed out of place at the Folies-Bergères and her horse, George, was equally dressed up to look the part. As Claire stripped off the layers, leaving a trail behind her, George kept going as if nothing untoward was occurring. Meanwhile, the audience was in stitches of laughter and wonderment. They got such an ovation that it almost raised the roof.

Carl Teike's famous march 'Old Comrades' formed the

background to a final parade of all the riders, ponies and horses who'd participated in the evening's entertainment. Afterwards, the chairman of the RDA, Jane Holderness-Rodham, presented each rider with a memento of the evening and we thanked her for the honour she had paid us by inviting us to perform. After the presentation, the riders stayed in the arena for a while so that people who were interested could come and talk to us. However, the hour was late and we needed to get enough rest to be able to compete in our two dressage classes the next day. Hopefully they would be as memorable as the evening had been. With Doug's help there were now six RDA disabled riders who had chosen to ride side-saddle, as well as the ones that I'd discovered, and most of us would be competing the next day. This was great news and made me all the more motivated to continue to assist these fine people.

The following week, I was invited to visit the group that Sarah rode with. I arrived, finding my way around the car park and stables, and met Sarah and the pony that she was riding. I was very anxious that her instructor and helpers knew how to handle and fit her side-saddle, which she had recently been given. It was a beautiful saddle, as is often the way, but it had been carelessly handled and not looked after well. I explained that this valuable thing, which was probably an antique, as many are, was difficult, if not impossible, to replace if it got dropped or damaged.

CHAPTER SEVENTEEN

The Birth of TRADISSAR RDA

With the success of the side-saddle spectacle at Hartpury, I was becoming more concerned with how I could develop this way of riding to make it more accessible to riders who wished to try it.

The RDA is a wonderful organisation and helps many riders with a disability to learn to ride, even if that simply gives fun and therapy. As I'd experienced, however, there was a noticeable knowledge gap for those riders who wished to do something different or wanted to improve their riding skills to compete at a higher level. I already had a handful of riders who had asked for my assistance. If I could become an RDA instructor, perhaps then I would comply with the safety standards and rules.

I visited a local group which was run by Elizabeth Gill and her friends. She was their senior advisor, a group instructor with some considerable years of experience. Elizabeth was very interested in what I wanted to do and was willing to get involved with the riders that came to School Farm.

While at Hartpury, Lyn Bennyson from the Shelley Centre for Therapeutic Riding, near Colchester, had spoken to me about paying a visit to their group with Lucky in tow and giving some side-saddle instruction. I was delighted and made a date to attend. There was going to be a round trip of some 280 miles, and they kindly offered to assist with the cost of transporting Lucky. I had kept in touch with Doug Smith and asked his advice on how to develop my plans further.

Roger, my transporter, was willing to go for several days so that I could combine the visit to the Shelley Centre with a couple of coaching sessions with Michel. There's nothing like killing two birds with one stone!

When we reached the Shelley Centre, Jane was on hand to help me and to plait up Lucky to make her look her best.

Lyn and Val, who were the key organisers, had invited some very special people for the day. They were all young riders who wanted to have a go at side-saddle, or had just taken an interest with a mind to trying it out in the future.

Lucky and I gave a display to music and I explained everything about what I was doing. We then invited riders to come and have a go. There was a tremendous line-up of excited boys and girls – so many, in fact, that to fit them all in and not disappoint anyone meant we could only give them a ten-to-fifteen-minute ride each. Lucky was marvellous, so patient and relaxed despite the clamouring of little people all around her. I sat in my wheelchair on the mounting block so that I could help each rider on to my little side-saddle. None of them had tried this before, but they all took it in their stride. Kids learn so fast and are generally rather fearless these days.

I should mention here that Lyn and her team had put their heads on the block by inviting Lucky and me to do this event. They were even supportive enough to suggest that I could use their riders in order to gain some teaching experience.

We were now seriously pushing the RDA boundaries of rules and regulations. They, like me, came under the control of a pretty formidable regional chairman. I had already felt the fury of mine over what they saw as my 'unrealistic ambitions'.

Lyn had a young rider named Zoe, aged ten, who had experienced a terrible accident that had left her paraplegic and totally unable to walk. She was keen to ride side-saddle so a local SSA member had loaned her a little one to fit Prince, the pony that she rode. This brave little girl was gobsmacked at seeing what Lucky and I had achieved and had high hopes of getting there herself.

That summer, and for the best part of a year, I became a member of the Shelley Group. I spent two days a week working there as a trainee instructor. I had about half a dozen naughty boys, who came from a school that specialised in enrolling children with behaviour and development problems. Their ages ranged from ten to twelve years, but some of them had a mental age well below this. They were great fun and would fight to have me take notice of them, often all at once. Some days they could be very challenging, but I didn't mind as this kept me on my toes. There was always help at hand if I got things in a bit of a tangle, as can often happen with a bunch of exuberant boys on horses. They loved playing team games, and on more than one occasion I became befuddled as to which direction this or that team should be going in. One such incident of confusion brought the wrath of my examiner down on me! All told, I did almost double the twenty hours that one must teach in order to pass as a group instructor (GI).

During that long, cold winter I journeyed each week to the Shelley Centre. Kind Margaret and John Fowler took me in. They gave me my own room and bathroom, and I quite literally became one of the family. They developed into the kindest of friends. Margaret was very involved at the riding centre and John was the vicar of St Mary's Church in Stoke-by-Nayland. It is one of the great churches of Suffolk, with a history to match its magnificence as a Grade I listed building. I used to love the long conversations I held with John on Christian values and other spiritual matters. It was usually over breakfast or during the evenings, although John was then the cook rather than the priest.

I also joined my friends at Shelley to attend training days, usually two or three times a year. These were mandatory for all the instructors and many of the helpers. They were usually held at other centres and would be organised by the county chairperson. One afternoon I was making the three-hour journey in the pouring rain. Soon three hours turned into four, and I was still trawling my way up the A14. I was becoming worried that I'd be late as I was guest of honour for the evening's events.

As I was driving down a country lane I came to a sharp bend with a torrent of water flowing across it. It was very difficult to see in the dark, with the rain pouring down as it was, but as I hit this stream, probably going faster than I should have been, I was thrown into a skid right across the road, through a fence and into a stand of trees, where I was halted most abruptly. Oh, hell! Within minutes a neighbour had heard the crash and was by my side with a torch. They couldn't believe my bad luck and were absolute kindness personified. They dragged my wheelchair out of the boot and somehow managed to salvage me and all my gear from my car, which, by the way, was a write-off.

John was phoned and had to leave the do and drive for nearly an hour to find me. It was too late for anything except to take me to his home and to let Bill know the good news that I was unharmed and safe. The next day he too had to make the journey along the A14 and country lanes to pick me up and take me home.

I made one more special trip to see my friends at Shelley, this time to attend the group's Christmas carol service. Thankfully I got there safely and on time, and it was yet another memorable event. I met one more special friend at the centre by the name of Ruth. Like me, she was a disabled rider who had had polio – we were kindred spirits. She was very interested in riding side-saddle, so I invited her to come and stay with Bill and me. Ruth would regularly join us for a few days at a time and ride Lucky side-saddle. Eventually she would end up joining my RDA group.

CHAPTER EIGHTEEN

An RDA Committee Is Formed

All this time we knew we had an ally in Doug Smith, for he had been supportive in every one of my activities thus far. No one knew at this stage where or in what direction my experience and dreams would take me. It was Bill's idea to form a committee of the friends who had been encouraging me.

He booked a conference room at a nice hotel in Oxford. This seemed a reasonable halfway house for most people to travel to. Those who sat around the table enjoying a sandwich lunch were Bill, myself, Doug Smith, Elizabeth Gill, our bank manager Richard Fook, and Jane Sauer – just enough people to form an RDA committee. I really wanted to invite Anthony Head, the actor, to be our patron as he was already fairly involved with the RDA and handed out the prizes at the nationals. It was unanimous that Doug should approach him on our behalf, and we were delighted when he accepted our invitation. He definitely helped to raise our profile on more than one occasion. Next, we needed someone eminent from the SSA, and Cindy Sims was a strong choice. Cindy is an international judge and instructor, and, like Bill and me, she lives in Hampshire. She also comes from a long line of side-saddle riders. She ticked all the boxes and we were honoured when she accepted our invitation to join our motley group. She would go on to give us countless hours of her time.

This was the first of many meetings that eventually led to the establishment of our official RDA group. It was Bill's suggestion that we call our group TRADISSAR, a clever acronym standing for Training the Disabled in Side-Saddle Riding.

CHAPTER NINETEEN

Welcome, Quob

Back to business as usual, and it was time to enter the South Bucks regionals again. Bill came running over to me as I was warming up Lucky for my test. He told me he had been talking to a lady called Anne Coney, who seemed to be another ally, and he wanted me to immediately go and introduce myself. Goodness! Lucky wasn't going too well and needed more warm-up time; however, meeting Anne seemed more important at that moment. I rode over to meet her in a field where she was about to judge young riders doing their country-skills riding tests. It was a brief meeting, but we had made a friend who would be a key player in setting up our own RDA group.

Lucky and I didn't qualify that year, for some reason. I'd made the nationals twelve years on the trot, so maybe this was a sign to hang up my boots and start in another direction.

Meanwhile, my disabled friend Zeb had been scouting out many of the equestrian establishments in the Hampshire area and was impressed with a riding school called Quob Stables. It had excellent facilities, with horses which could be made available to us, and the owner, Beth Boyne, was keen to have an RDA group using her premises.

Before leaving School Farm, Zeb, who was always inspirational, had contacted Meridian television and asked them to come and see us. Richard Sley, their top presenter, turned up with a cameraman. Elizabeth Gill and several riders were there to meet them. Richard's first question was "Where are the disabled people?" Zeb rattled off the names and disabilities of each one of us and his manner changed. They interviewed us, and Zeb and I gave a little demonstration riding side-saddle on Lucky, which they were impressed with. Meridian News gave us some very nice coverage of our activities and dreams to form an RDA group. Lady Fairfield, the admiral's wife, heard about our work and liked very much what we were doing. She managed to convince her friend, Sir Donald Gosling, one of the co-founders of National Car Parks (NCP), to give us a very generous donation.

We said a sad farewell to School Farm and hastily moved Lucky and all our gear to Quob Stables, in Durley. Within no time at all we had eight disabled riders training with us, half of them riding side-saddle. Beth was quick to pick up on the necessary side-saddle techniques and soon added them to the skills that her riding school could offer. Her daughter had also taken to riding Lucky side-saddle, and wanted to ride her own horse that way. To facilitate all this additional interest I invited Liz Turner, a long-time leading figure in the SSA, to come to Quob and bring some side-saddles with her. Liz turned up with a trolley load of lovely side-saddles. She fitted out two horses: one on Beth's daughter's horse and the other on a riding-school horse.

One of Quob's instructors was Philippa, and she was also keen to learn. She made rapid progress riding with Lucky, and it was decided that she would be Quob's official side-saddle instructor. At this stage of TRADISSAR there was very little in the coffers and no income to speak of, so Beth very kindly offered to hold an event to raise some money for our charity.

I dressed in my Duchess of Gordon outfit as the 'Chief of the Gordon Highlanders', a regiment that she raised to fight in the Napoleonic Wars. I rode to some Scottish music by Jimmy Shand, and during my performance I threw out handfuls of

Harrod's chocolate coins into the audience for the boys and girls to catch and eat.

Coming up to my final salute, my busby caught a breeze and came loose, falling embarrassingly down my back. I was now hatless, but fortunately it didn't drop beyond my shoulders as it was attached with elastic. They were a most appreciative audience and we raised about £400 for TRADISSAR. Thank you, Beth!

Quob gave our riders the use of a small undercover area, and at times we could even use the main school when it wasn't being used for other lessons.

Under Elizabeth's supervision, I was able to instruct our riders myself. With her support we were now a lot closer to becoming an official RDA group. Little did we know that Anne, who was on the RDA board of directors, had arranged to have the constitution changed. Before this it was almost impossible for any new group to be formed. Anne was also successful in persuading the county chairman and instructors to support me.

The weeks passed and as our numbers grew we needed to engage more helpers. Their duties would include saddling up the horses, including Lucky; looking after them before, during and after the ride; assisting the riders to mount and dismount; leading them around if required; and just being at the riders' sides to encourage them. We recruited a number of people from the staff and liveries who had their own horses stabled at Quob. It was Elizabeth's responsibility to train these people, ensure their references were in order and also to liaise with the police in order to carry out a CRB (Criminal Records Bureau) check. Once our team of assistants was in place and functioning, Elizabeth considered it timely to invite Anne down to see us at work.

Our long-running negotiations with the RDA were close to bearing fruit. A date was set for November and a high-powered delegation headed by Mrs Anne Coney, the regional chairman, and the chief instructors descended on Quob. They checked that all the facilities met with RDA standards and rigorously inspected our classes to ensure we provided the correct level of tuition and support for disabled people. They declared TRADISSAR fit for purpose and ratified the official creation of our RDA group, specialising in side-saddle for the disabled. At last, after two years of gruelling effort, everything was in place. We aspired to become a centre of excellence.

One of our star riders was twenty-seven-year-old Sarah Piercy. Sarah was born with a condition called arthrogryposis, which affects most of her joints, even her jaw, and has stunted her growth. As a result she spends most of her time in a wheelchair. She also has learning difficulties and attended a school for people with special needs. During her time there she was offered horse riding as a therapy, an offer she took up eagerly. However, owing to the restricted movement of her hips and limbs, she found riding astride difficult and painful and made little progress. Despite her problems, Sarah is a determined and courageous person – she won the London wheelchair marathon in 2000 and has competed a further seven times. Upon discovering side-saddle a few years ago she realised that this method of riding gave her a chance to excel. She was introduced to Lucky and me, and advanced so rapidly that she was part of my side-saddle display at the national championships' evening performance. Sarah lived in Exeter and had to travel to Southampton on a regular basis so she could benefit from TRADISSAR's offerings.

Zeb is a mother of two girls, the younger of whom still lives at home. Zeb is seriously dyslexic, and has other learning difficulties as well. At school her problems were not understood; this resulted in clinical depression, making it difficult for her to find satisfactory employment. She won a Prince of Wales Award, however, and studied reiki, a

Japanese therapy used for the healing of both humans and animals. Passionate about all life, she is gifted at treating horses suffering from emotional and physical damage. Owing to hip problems that developed after the birth of her second daughter, much to her distress, Zeb found that riding astride had become increasingly difficult and painful. She had almost reached the point of giving up riding altogether when she was introduced to me and she became a dear, close friend.

We spent a memorable weekend away at a para-dressage qualifier in Gloucestershire. Not only did we stay up talking half the night, but we laughed the whole weekend. Then we had to negotiate our way home through terrific floods that hit Gloucestershire over the weekend. It was more by good luck than management that we found our way through and reached home safely. I would often ask her advice about Lucky's well-being and she would give an honest judgement that I would take seriously. She is a successful equine reiki master practitioner who travels frequently to the United States to teach others her skills.

CHAPTER TWENTY

Quob and Beyond

We functioned at Quob for a year, our membership growing steadily and soon becoming skilled enough to ride independently. The little school was now too small to accommodate more than two advanced riders at a time, and if we used the big arena we had to share it with the liveries who would come in to exercise and school their horses. These horses were sometimes a little exuberant and came too close to our not-so-confident riders, making them feel a little vulnerable. It was decided that these facilities weren't quite meeting our needs for safety. Once again our excellent scout Zeb went on another reconnaissance mission. She came back with the good news that Crofton Manor Equestrian Centre in Fareham, Hampshire, was willing to have us. Kevin Ward, the proprietor, had given his blessing and Karen, who was the manager of the riding school, would look after us.

Monday was the horses' day off after a usually busy working weekend. Elizabeth, Zeb and I hotfooted it to Crofton Manor to see if it was indeed a suitable venue for TRADISSAR's growing needs. Kevin was welcoming and showed us the horses that we could use, as well as the indoor school. The school and stables were all under the same roof, which made it very convenient, especially in cold and wet weather. It seemed ideal for our purpose, but it was some distance further to travel for a few of our members and we sadly had to part ways.

There was one other problem with Crofton. All of the liveries were DIY yards – an issue I'd never faced before – and not attached to the main school. If Lucky was to move here I wouldn't be able to take care of her myself; I would need to hire grooms to look after her daily needs. The people at Crofton were very supportive and helpful, and took care of Lucky for the next nine years. We tried a number of grooms who turned out to be unsatisfactory, but dear, loyal Selina, who looked after her daughter's pony in the stable opposite, and her daughter Daisy, would lovingly care for Lucky in all weathers and even once or twice when I was unable to be there due to illness.

The premises had to be inspected for safety by the county chairman and instructor, but they quickly gave their approval. As well as stabling Lucky, Crofton agreed to let us make use of the school facilities every Monday. Once we'd moved everything in, we started our new life at Crofton and quickly adjusted to the different travelling times and the new horses there. Our first duty, each Monday, was to tidy the school and clean up after the busy weekend activities. This was our way of contributing to the school's maintenance. We weren't charged for the use of the facilities, only the horses that we used.

The riders who transferred included Sarah, Zeb, Maeve, Caroline, Penny, and Ruth when she could make it. Penny and Maeve were our longest-standing members and the first to help us get organised as a group. Both ladies were diagnosed with multiple sclerosis (MS) and both suffered with relapsing symptoms, but enjoyed the benefits that the riding gave them. Like me, the horses gave them the freedom from not having to struggle with the difficulties that being on terra firma brings. Both ladies needed a lot of help, and Maeve's friend Amber stepped into the breach, understanding their needs immediately. Amber was a keen horsewoman herself, and is still competing at dressage.

These were quickly followed by a new novice rider called Debbie, who had been recommended to us by Cindy. We called her 'Bionic' because most of her spine was held together with metal implants. Lucky taught her the finer points of riding, and within eighteen months of coaching she was talent-spotted for the Paralympic National Dressage Team. Next came Danny, Jemma, Liz and Christina. Christina had heard good things about us and travelled over from the Isle of Wight each week. Christina was a ten-year-old bright young lady. She had cerebral palsy and was partially sighted, but she wanted to do side-saddle. Lucky was still our only side-saddle horse, but fortunately my little side-saddle was suitable for Christina to use on her. She would be led mostly, but it is remarkable how quickly the blind can adjust to their surroundings and she quickly became independent. After some time, Liz Turner and I visited Christina's Isle of Wight group and Liz was able to fit Christina's pony with a suitable side-saddle. I hope that she is still making use of it.

Jemma also chose to ride Lucky side-saddle as her 'bionic' knees made it difficult to sit in the normal manner. Over the years she was successful in passing all the grades, I to IV, in riding and horse care and also won a bronze certificate on Lucky. This was quite remarkable considering Jemma's dyslexia and learning difficulties.

With the move to Crofton we had to engage and train up more helpers, and we now needed more instructors to take some of the load off Elizabeth. I was concentrating on the side-saddle riders, and Cindy Sims, our president and a side-saddle expert, rolled up her sleeves and became a great asset to us.

In less than six months we had two willing helpers who seemed prepared to put in the time and training to take on more responsibility. They were called Helen and Greer. They both owned and rode their own horses. Helen bravely took on board the responsibility of being a logbook holder, which set out the duties that she must fulfil – i.e. the number of hours each week she instructed, and the number of riders in her group. She would have to plan her lessons each week and then evaluate and report on the riders progress. Greer was an ex-schoolteacher and, though we would have liked her to also take on a logbook, she preferred to be an organiser and at this she was brilliant. The horses respected her and she took no nonsense from the kids; everything just ran like clockwork when she was in charge. Valuable people!

We were fortunate to have some other teenagers who were keen helpers. Under some supervision from Greer, they could groom and tack up the horses and ponies that we'd been using. They were also willing walkers, leading the riders around the school sometimes for several hours at a time.

We desperately needed another side-saddle horse and were lucky to find Yeoman, an ex-police horse and a gentleman, who took to side-saddle like a duck to water.

When Ellen Chapman, a blind and physically limited rider, joined us she really took to Yeoman. He reciprocated and was able to look after her needs. She was accompanied by a carer who would eventually become her husband – yet another success story!

Two more remarkable riders joined us – Amy and Shelley. Amy was something of a challenge, even for us. She was blind, had terrible epileptic fits, and had a brain condition which was terminal. This brave sixteen-year-old young lady rode with us most weeks for many months. Her favourite mount was Joy, a skewbald cob, who was popular with several other riders. Amy had a big day when Anne Coney came to see us in her role as examiner. We had prepared three riders to do their grade-I riding and horse-care tests. They all passed, but Amy was the only candidate to be put forward for a grade-II assessment and she nailed that as well! It was a very full and exciting day, culminating in a plethora of photo opportunities and a round of tea and cakes.

Shelley was a mother of three children, but sadly they had been taken into care at some stage and eventually went to live with their father. Shelley was being treated for depression and had a severe back problem which needed surgery to deal with the pain that she was having. She was a fairly experienced rider and was thrilled to ride Lucky. She did both side-saddle and cross-saddle, going through all the grade tests, I to IV, in no time at all, animal care and riding, eventually being successful in passing the Bronze Certificate in both. She also took on the responsibilities of a helper and went on to became our next group instructor (GI), able to take on some of the more advanced riders. Shelley blossomed within the group, becoming a committee member and often assessing horses and their suitability for our use. Her teenage son, Michael, was also among our young volunteers. Within a few years Shelley's family were reunited with her and she had two more little babies. She considers herself another TRADISSAR success story.

CHAPTER TWENTY-ONE

Kevin

Still in our first year at Crofton, I was approached by a lady and gentleman from social services. They asked me if I would be willing to take on a fourteen-year-old named Kevin who had serious behavioural and learning problems, but also a love of horses. They thought that I might be able to channel this passion in order to allay some of his bad behaviour. He had wonderful parents, who had adopted him and his twin sister when they were aged two. However, it seemed that they had found it difficult to manage them, hence the reason for them being in care and for social services to be involved. I am sympathetic to anyone in need of some assistance, especially if they have a passion for animals and particularly – as in Kevin's case – horses. I knew from experience what an animal can do to change a person's life, so I took Kevin on and social services agreed to work with me.

I was in Lucky's stable preparing her for work when Kevin arrived with his carer, Michael, who suffered from MS. Michael doubled up as one of our volunteer helpers until his condition worsened and he wasn't able to lead the horses around the school without becoming unduly fatigued.

Kevin was tall, good-looking and chatty, and without an invitation entered Lucky's stable and went straight over to introduce himself with pats and strokes. We were taken aback by this 'love at first sight' reaction between an animal and a human being. As I began to tack up and put the side-saddle on Lucky, Kevin wanted to know all about it.

"Would you like to try?" I asked.

He was up for anything to do with Lucky, and so it was decided that Kevin should ride side-saddle right from the start. Later, when Anne Coney asked Kevin why he chose to ride side-saddle, he answered simply, "Because it's safe."

Kevin was a willing helper and had bags of energy. This was not always easy to channel as he could be there one minute and vanish the next, no doubt up to some mischief or other. It wasn't long before we realised that he had a penchant for other people's mobile phones and money. We had to dismiss him at one stage over stealing a lot of money from TRADISSAR. Bill and I worked with the authorities for some time after this incident, but eventually he was reinstated. Being denied the joy of riding was punishment enough. This teenager was responsive to the interest and friendship that Bill and I gave him and I got many invitations to tea and supper at Kevin's home. He was a natural actor, taking on the role of cook and waiter, and treated me with all the elegance and good manners of a professional – how sweet! His mentors were always proud of his behaviour. As he got older, we realised that when he reached his eighteenth birthday he would be thrown out of the care system into the big wide world. We needed to think carefully about a career that he could focus on. I contacted the British Racing School in Newmarket and spoke to the principal of the Jockey School. He graciously invited us to come and meet them. Over the course of a two-day visit Kevin was shown every aspect of jockey training, from riding the galloping mechanical horses to seeing the apprentice jockeys taking their morning exercises. After several interviews and assessments it was decided that perhaps Kevin wasn't suited to the life of a jockey, as it was physically and mentally taxing. Instead I suggested that he could benefit from a programme offered by the Fortune Centre of Riding Therapy, located in the New Forest. They offer a three-year certificated programme for teenagers with physical and/or learning disabilities to gain the skills required to work and care for horses. Kevin was still able to attend our Monday sessions until he graduated. As his final farewell to TRADISSAR he performed a sponsored display on Lucky, while dressed in his pyjamas. Kevin's humour, of course – what fun! He raised over £150 for our charity; what a commitment and what a success story!

CHAPTER TWENTY-TWO

Summertime at Crofton

Each summer for six weeks, from July until the end of August, Crofton Manor Riding School would hire out their horses and facilities to riding students from France. They would come across in groups and stay in England for two weeks per team. Part of their programme was to ride every day, meaning we couldn't use our usual horses for our riders. That didn't stop us from going about our normal activities, and it was quite remarkable how we kept going in spite of this hindrance. Poor Lucky had to work overtime on Mondays, but she was always rewarded by being given extra time off to recuperate. A number of our riders owned their horses and would bring them to Crofton to keep up with their training. The ponies were available, for the most part, so the young riders were still well catered for.

With the onset of better weather the most popular activity for everyone was to head into the fresh air and sunshine and hack out around the extensive fields at Crofton.

We took on an education programme set out by ASDAN (Award Scheme Development and Accreditation Network) in horse riding, horse care and stable management. This was a detailed curriculum which was different from the RDA grade tests, although in many ways the two overlapped. Susan Jones would come over from time to time to guide us through all the different modules and activities. We worked on two levels: 'Transition Challenge' and 'Towards Independence' for the more advanced riders. Some of the subjects covered by these courses included preparing the housing for the animal; feeding and healthcare; grooming; providing the animal with an interesting and stimulating environment; animal and animal-handler safety, etc. This was all excellent material, and the students would have to show evidence that they had fully covered these activities by attaching diagrams and photos, etc., to their workbooks.

Not only were there ongoing education programmes for our riders, but there were many training days necessary for our instructors and helpers. These sessions could be taught 'in house' or off site at another RDA centre. We would have to make our own way to the centres, sometimes over a considerable distance, and it could take up most of the day. My committee would help me arrange our own training programmes, sometimes by inviting a visitor to share their understanding in particular areas where we needed to improve our skills or knowledge. Cindy Sims, our president, was a favourite in this regard because her experience was so vast. Our regional and county instructors were also helpful in ensuring we maintained the high standards required by the RDA.

One of the most interesting visits was to the Loddon School, near Hook in Hampshire. This was a special school for young people, in particular those with autism and those whose communication skills were severely handicapped. They also used riding as part of their therapies and, along with a large assortment of animals, we were introduced to their two donkeys. These animals formed a big part of the boys' and girls' activities. Most of these people required one-to-one tuition from their teacher/carer. The carers were all highly trained and it was a rich experience for us to see them in action. We also made a reciprocal visit to the Rainbow Centre for people with disabilities and special needs, following a visit by their organisers to TRADISSAR.

CHAPTER TWENTY-THREE

Matilda

One Monday morning, myself and several of my loyal helpers arrived to assist in the general clear-up and tidying of the indoor school and facilities that we used at Crofton. However, we found the premises in total chaos and were given the news that the centre had been burgled. All the staff were adamant that the place had been left in reasonable order and safety the evening before. The school had been broken into, vandalised and most of the office equipment, including the computer, had gone. In addition to this, TRADISSAR's electric scooter had gone missing. We were all numb with shock at the situation, though fortunately none of the horses seemed to have been tampered with. I was determined that our plight should be known far and wide, on the off chance that making it public might turn up some witnesses. The local police constabulary had been contacted and I phoned our local newspaper. They sent Chris Broon, a local journalist, out to see us with a cameraman. We had met Chris before, when we wanted his help to publicise other events, so he was already on our side. He did us proud, and wrote a great story about the break-in and the terrible loss to us as a charity.

The next day Chris's half-page article, accompanied by some photos, came out in the *Portsmouth News*. That same day Bill and I received twelve phone calls before lunchtime from people offering to replace our scooter. We couldn't believe the wonderful response from the public and the outrage they expressed about the incident. The first of these calls came from Michael Lane, who along with his eighty-eight-year-old mother, Lawrie, had read Chris's article. Michael explained that his mother had a scooter sitting in the garage which she hoped to be able to use again sometime in the future. Sadly she had recently had a stroke and felt it would be more appreciated and serve a better purpose elsewhere. So it was that the scooter, dubbed Matilda, a name that we retained, was delivered to Crofton for the grateful use of TRADISSAR RDA. A couple of days after the burglary the stolen scooter, now severely damaged, was discovered about a mile away. According to the police report, the joyriders must have ridden it until they got sick of it and then vandalised it for good measure.

Matilda was not only used to get our disabled students around Crofton. She went on many other journeys – to the regional and national championships, on training days, and to London in 2012 for the Paralympics. Bill and the committee would regularly arrange fun days out for the children, including one to Marwell Zoo, where Matilda was in attendance once more. Everyone took turns riding her around. Several of the children wanted to be driver, either sitting on an adult's knees or standing up if they were tall enough. When TRADISSAR had no more use for her she was donated to the local Mobility charity shop, where Maeve, one of our long-standing members, used to work as a volunteer. It's nice to know that Matilda still remains among loving, caring friends.

The costume to beat all costumes – Rayna as Charles I's young wife,
Henrietta Maria, riding on Star.

Becky on her new horse, riding 'off' side-saddle, Rayna on Star, in the pairs at the SSA, 2005.

Lucky winning her first RDA nationals.

The RDA nationals 2006 – Claire Lewis, Rayna Matthews, Paula Keely and Helen Hogarth. The first item in the evening's entertainment: a quadrille to music.

Tilly Shepherd and Rayna on Lucky after the entertainment.

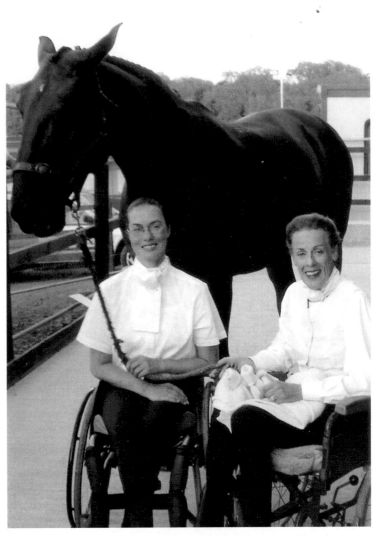

Sarah Piercy and Rayna.

Zeb on Lucky.

Ruth on Lucky.

Introducing

TRADISSAR

(TRAining the DIsabled
in Side-SAddle Riding)

Registered Charity No. 1117937

TRADISSAR booklet cover.

Penny with Paul.

Rayna at the Shelley Centre.

Tia on Fern.

Sophie on Travis.

Edwina on Lucky.

Debbie on Yeoman.

Belinda with Shelley and Annie.

Sasha on Lucky with our second instructor, Shelley.

Mason on Fern.

Deborah Miller on Yeoman.

Jemma Salmon – Bronze Certificate.

Ellen Chapman, one of our blind riders, on Lucky,
with her carer and husband.

Edwina Le May, disabled side-saddle rider.

Belinda.

Midge Bainbridge, County Physio, at tea after an assessment with riders and helpers, including Caroline, Amy, Maeve, Mo, and Rayna,

Amy, with instructor Helen and Yeoman.

TRADISSAR volunteers at tea.

Liam Travers on Diva.

CHAPTER TWENTY-FOUR

Countrywide

One day, we were contacted by the local Totton branch of Countrywide. They are a chain of fifty stores, scattered across the country, and are well known for their charitable activities. Each shop would spend several days throughout the year having fundraising drives. I was quick to welcome the opportunity to be involved in these days and enlisted as many of TRADISSAR's members as possible to help the staff sell their cakes and take donations from the customers. This was also a great opportunity for us to increase public awareness for our project. We would hang up our banners in the stores and chat with the customers about our ongoing work and achievements.

That year, the national manager of Countrywide's alternate feeds, Charles Duf of West Wellow, Hampshire, also a long-distance cyclist, decided to spend his holidays doing a national cycling tour of all fifty Countrywide branches. This amounted to a round trip of 1,125 miles! He would need to ride 100 miles per day, rain, hail or shine. The day he arrived at the Totton branch the gardening guru and former *Ground Force* presenter Charlie Dimmock and I were waiting to congratulate him. Charles looked the part in his cycling gear and rode what appeared to be a rather fine machine. He had time for one delicious piece of cake and a quick drink before he had to be on his way again. He was hoping to raise £25,000 for the RDA for the third consecutive year.

The year 2012 was an exciting one and a time of considerable change for TRADISSAR. Towards the end of the year we were told that Kevin Ward was planning on closing the riding school, but we were reassured that we would be able to continue as usual. Their horses were gradually being sold off, but very fortunately for us many of the horses that we used in our classes were bought by people who continued to keep them at Crofton. We were able to persuade their new owners to let us continue to use them for our riders on Mondays. In many cases the new owners were pleased that we were keeping them well trained and mannered, and in several instances we helped to pay for some of the horses' expenses in return for their use.

This was also the year of the Paralympic Games in London. We perused the programme for riders we'd most like to see compete and decided that Monday 4 September was the best day to attend. We hired a coach so that we would have room for all members who wished to share in the spectacle. We had to get up at the crack of dawn to make correct time from Crofton, but fortunately it was a light and fine day.

It was almost a four-hour journey into London, winding through the South Bank streets to the Olympic Stadium. On arrival we were all brimming with excitement. We found excellent seating and positions to see our equestrian friends riding their tests in the massive arena. We witnessed the high-profile riders, the grade IIIs and IVs, who had won their way through to the finals. The response from the thousands-strong crowd in the grandstands was rather unique. People stood up and sat down in silent unison, making great Mexican waves which continued from grandstand to grandstand right around the arena. This was such an effective way of applauding without scaring the sensitive horses.

It was not an easy job to round up all our members, children, buggies and gear, and make our way back through a great throng of happy people to find our coach. When we finally made it back to Crofton it was way past most of our bedtimes.

CHAPTER TWENTY-FIVE

Post-Paralympics

The experience had a profound effect on my riders and they were ever more eager to 'up' their riding skills in order to compete. This actually wasn't an option when using riding-school horses, because we couldn't compete on them or, indeed, ride them anywhere except Crofton, but we could now see more exciting avenues open to us.

The RDA were holding a competition in October, not long after the Paralympics, which included an event called Dressage Anywhere. This was certainly something we could aim for, so we began to make preparations. The date of the event was set for Monday 24 October, and we made arrangements for our riders to enter. Each test would be judged online, so we needed a video camera and an excellent cameraman. Susie Flook, one of our generous sponsors, made a camera available to us and Jo, one of our riders, would manage the technology. Each rider and test would be recorded and then uploaded to the Internet for judging by the RDA.

There were several tests, of varying difficulty, that would suit each rider. Over the next few weeks our riders chose a specific test or tests and worked hard at perfecting their skills. This was an opportunity for Lucky to shine, and Diane Pettet, who had been riding for some years now, wanted to do a 'walk and trot' test and then the more advanced 'walk and trot and canter' test for good measure. Vanessa Palmer had also been riding Lucky on a regular basis, and she wanted to compete in the 'walk and trot' test as well. Vanessa had had a stroke, affecting her right side, which meant that she controlled Lucky with her left hand using a split-bar rein. Lucky was definitely the most trustworthy mount for them to ride as she knew them both well and had plenty of experience competing at all levels. Debbie Miller, who usually rode side-saddle, said that she preferred to ride her own horse, Memphis, in the 'walk and trot' test. Tia, our little junior star, wasn't going to be outdone by the adult ladies and wanted to show us what she could do. To ensure her safety we decided to put her on a leading-rein pony. As this was all going to be judged online, this competition would be performed in the Crofton competition dressage arena.

The day soon arrived – horses were washed and plaited up and both mounts and riders were looking their very best. We gave each rider half an hour to warm up and then they rode their test or tests through two or three times in front of the camera. It was then my job to choose the best performance to be sent off for judging.

When the scores and percentages were returned to us we were blown away by the results. All four riders had qualified for the national championships, getting scores well up in the 60s and early 70s percentile ranges. Wow!

The nationals were held in March, so we had a few months to practise before the next set of Dressage Anywhere tests needed to be recorded. We sent them off to be judged and, again, the results were still good – Di came in second place for her grade-III 'walk, trot and canter' test, and Vanessa came fourth in the 'walk and trot' test. Oh, we were so proud of our riders in what was to be the first of many competitions. The next year everyone was very keen to have another go at Dressage Anywhere – all four of last year's riders put themselves forward and Jo and Liz joined the team on their own horses.

Lots of practice was done for this new round of tests, and we tried each rider out on a variety of horses to make sure they got the best performance partnership. The results of this regional competition were once again encouraging, and Di and Jo qualified for the nationals. Jo went on to win her class with a terrific score of 79.78%, landing herself a gold medal and some fantastic Carl Hester classic reins. The reaction to this wonderful news was floods of happy tears. Jo was a rather special case for TRADISSAR. She came to us with a prosthetic left leg, from the knee joint down, as a result of diabetes, begging to be taken on as a disabled rider. Not a problem, we said, but sadly Jo had some weight concerns which we had to take into serious consideration. Not to be beaten, and because of her love of horses and all things equestrian, she became a loyal and well-trusted helper. She progressed into being a logbook holder and also took on the responsibility of instructing some of our more challenging riders. Over time Jo lost over four and a half stone in weight, bringing her within the weight regulation to ride Alfi. He did her proud and she brought home our second set of Carl Hester classic reins by winning test four.

Things at TRADISSAR were moving towards competing at a serious level and the students' ambitions were growing. The next challenge would be to compete at the regional championships at South Bucks. Following on from my years of experience at these events, I was delighted for all involved.

We had some time before the regionals to arrange some more serious training for our riders. At a judges' training day I had the opportunity to explain our current position to Waveney Luke, an RDA dressage judge and the organiser of many judge and para-training days. She was always looking out for new and potentially talented disabled riders.

By this time Vanessa had her own horse and was anxious to continue competing. She was delighted to be invited to one of Waveney's training days with her chestnut mare and she gained a lot of insight and experience. I asked Waveney if we could hold a talent-spotting training day at Crofton Manor and got an enthusiastic response from her. For our riders to get the full benefit of such an opportunity we needed to ask Kevin's permission to hire the indoor school that was used for all the competitions. Kevin was more than happy for us to utilise the facilities for a day, and he gave us a considerable price reduction. How fortunate we were! An arena twenty by forty metres was measured out, with all the boundary boards and lettering in the correct places. The level of excitement was rising rapidly.

The big day was on a Thursday in February and Simon Laurens was picked to be the coach. Waveney would attend as well, and we had eight riders looking forward to the day. Our journalist friend from the newspaper was invited to come in the hope that he could provide Crofton and TRADISSAR RDA with some publicity. Simon arrived early, followed by Waveney, and they had a full day's work ahead of them if each rider was to have forty minutes' individual coaching time.

Lucky and her riders opened the proceedings, and praise was given for the way she was still able to perform at the highest para-level. Jo was thrilled to be given a chance to show what she and Alfi could do.

Debbie wanted to ride Yeoman, side-saddle, and also get some advice for riding her own horse, Memphis. She was very pleased to have a gold-medal-winning trainer available to give her some new tips.

Likewise, Vanessa wanted her mare, Kiwi, to get some extra help from an expert; but she also wanted to spend time riding Lucky, so we arranged for her to do both.

Several other riders found the day most stimulating. Ever enthusiastic, our star rider, Tia, now eight years old, wanted to join in on her favourite mount, Fern. We'd recently switched her Pony Pilch side-saddle to a more traditional one, and now she really looked the part.

Both Waveney and Simon were unanimous in their evaluation of our riders; they declared that they were all of potential para-talent and that we could attend any of their training days in the future. This was great news, and arrangements were made by Waveney to have a follow-up day at Crofton in April.

CHAPTER TWENTY-SIX

Newsletter

It was decided by our committee that we should produce our own newsletter. This decision coincided with a project called Life with Art – a charity founded by David Piggot, who was in the property business. The project involved the hosting of art exhibitions in unused residential, retail or industrial spaces, usually empty buildings or office blocks. These would then be opened to the public for viewing. One of these venues, called 1600, was in a business park near Fareham.

I was delighted by David's invitation to get involved with the programme. Two or three times a year, and running for six weeks at a time, I would assist with the set-up and daily running of an exhibition of beautifully produced photos depicting the everyday activities of an RDA centre.

My job was to manage the exhibition – opening the building to the public at certain times and ensuring everything was made secure at the end of each day. For this I received a small fee. This became a very welcome income to TRADISSAR over a number of years. I would spend many hours in 1600, and so I needed to put this time to good use. I would while away the hours by managing the TRADISSAR records, preparing for my judge listing exam, and planning the next week's riding and educational activities. It was a perk of the job that I was allowed to make use of the building for my own needs. It was ideal for meetings, social events, education programmes,

Christmas parties and more.

There was plenty of extra exhibition space on the premises, so I was able to create an additional display of my historical costumes.

Shirley Harris, who came to us as a helper and became a GI and committee member, used to join me on duty on occasions. We would put our heads together and compose our newsletter twice a year. All our activities at Life with Art at 1600, as well as all our rider and horsey pursuits, were considered newsworthy items and featured in the newsletter.

Waveney Luke continued to invite us to attend training days, usually at South Bucks. Several of our riders and horses were keen to take advantage of this opportunity. Even Tia was able to attend these; her school was very encouraging and allowed her the time away from her lessons to show off her side-saddle skills. Alfi, our big, chunky cob, was always a favourite with Clive. Di was heard to say, "I want one," such was his character; he had a wonderful temperament, the correct paces and was just ideal for an RDA mount.

Another newsworthy event was the Body Shop spring-cleaning. Susie visited us with her Body Shop staff for a volunteers' day out. The indoor school was in great need of a thorough clean-up and they rose to the challenge. The height of the school meant that a long reach was necessary, and as we didn't want anyone climbing ladders we purchased and modified some cleaning tools to allow us to get up into all the corners – well done, Bill. TRADISSAR volunteers also joined in with the cleaning and the indoor school looked so much better for their efforts.

Not only did TRADISSAR benefit from this clean-up, but the Crofton Manor Riding School stables did too. We always tried to go the extra mile for them as a special thank you for the use of their facilities. Bill and I sent a letter to Susie and her team of international lawyers from the Body Shop for giving their time so generously, and we received some positive and helpful feedback on the day.

By the tail end of the year we had raised enough money to purchase some special mirrors for the indoor school. These helped our riders, as well as the other riders at Crofton, to see what they looked like while riding and trying to improve on their skills. These mirrors were quite expensive as they needed to be accident-proof. Little did we know that they would be put to the test so soon. That January, one of the Crofton riders had an accident on her horse and crashed into one of the mirrors. It shattered, but no glass fell to the floor of the school. The mirror had performed exactly as promised. All the glass was contained by the special coating on it. Fortunately the rider suffered no serious injury, despite the impact. The mirror was expensive and we wondered how and when we would be able to afford another one. I phoned my sales contact, Andrea, at Mirrors4U to tell her what had happened. Within a few days she sent a replacement over, together with a team of fitters, and before we knew it we had a lovely new mirror. Thank you so much for your very generous gift.

Around this time we were told that Yeoman, our side-saddle horse, was too old and needed to be retired. We were sad to see him go, but wished him a well-earned, long and happy retirement. This meant that the hunt was on for another backup side-saddle horse for Lucky. The staff at Crofton suggested a horse named Drambuie. The side-saddle was tried out on him, and we thought that with a few minor adjustments all would be well. The saddler was duly called and Shelley volunteered to ride Drambuie while the modifications were made to ensure everything was fitted correctly.

Part of my responsibility to TRADISSAR was to continually improve my own skills as a trainer. I spent nearly three years trying to achieve the RDA's A certificate. During this time I spent many days and hours at various RDA centres, learning the skills required for instructing groups of riders. There were also many training days, and several times I made the six-hour journey to a centre in North Wales.

Once, I miraculously made the journey when most of England was snowbound. I reached Newbury in Hampshire to be told that all the transporters were grounded and all the main routes were closed. Very discouraged, I went in a McDonald's to have a hot drink. There I befriended two fellows also considering what their next move would be, and after hearing of my plight, they said, "Just follow us – we'll get you there."

I followed their little white van for mile upon mile, and after nearly three hours we reached the M6. They signed for me to continue and suddenly they were out of sight and I was on my way. What guardian angels had I met? I was the only candidate that arrived from the south of England for that training course.

I also attempted to be a UKCC coach, spending another few years on the course and many journeys to the Avon RDA, near Bristol. I was successful in two out of the three units that I needed to qualify, but sadly my disability meant I wasn't physically capable of coaching large groups. Nevertheless, I had learnt a great deal from my experiences and the time spent working towards these goals.

CHAPTER TWENTY-SEVEN

The Mayor of Fareham Visits

Susan Bayford, soon to be Mayor of Fareham, decided that we would be one of the Mayor's charities during her term in office and paid us a visit at Crofton. The Mayor chooses three charities each year and, as fundraising wasn't Bill's favourite occupation, we were grateful to be chosen and pledged to give her our full support.

Bill and I were invited to the 'Mayor-Making Ceremony' at Ferneham Hall in Fareham. It was a rather grand occasion, beginning with a civic luncheon. We met and talked to many members of Fareham Borough Council and associated social services. We learnt that Brian, Susan's consort, had also been mayor, in 2010/11, and so was able to pass on his advice and mayoral experiences to his wife.

The launch event for the Mayor's charities was held at the Rainbow Centre, another of her beneficiaries, the third one being the Royal Navy and Royal Marines Charity. I wasn't able to attend this day, as I was at the RDA regional championships with some of my riders, so Shirley and her husband Ralph joined Bill in my place. They learnt a lot of interesting information about these other two charities.

The Rainbow Centre in Fareham provided support not only for our local area, but for much further afield. They give a conductive education programme for children and adults with motor disabilities (such as cerebral palsy and stroke survivors), which helps to improve their mobility and independence.

The third charity was one dear to the hearts of Susan and Brian as they had both served in the naval forces. The Royal Navy and Royal Marines Charity supports and funds both serving and retired members of both organisations, and their families, in times of hardship and disaster.

On another visit to Crofton, Susan brought a photographer with her. We had lots of fun posing for our pictures to be taken, riders and horses included. On seeing our magnificent side-saddle horse, Magnus, Susan said that she would like to have a go – how sporting is that? Magnus is a gentle giant, an eighteen-hand Clydesdale, and they looked rather comical with Susan perched on top of him, riding side-saddle while dressed in all her Mayor's finery.

Barclays Bank in Fareham's main shopping centre held a fundraising day which we became involved with. We were encouraged to advertise ourselves by hanging our TRADISSAR banner and exhibiting one of my historical costumes along with a side-saddle on a stand. Quite a few of us turned up on the day to offer customers tea or coffee, with cakes, in return for donations. We mingled among the thin crowd, and business seemed quite slow until Tia and her mother arrived. Then things really took off. This eight-year-old girl captivated everyone – she took matters into her own hands and the office turned into a friendly 'café'. She was shrewd enough not to let anyone leave without first giving something to her charity tin. At the end of the day she had extracted some hundreds of pounds for TRADISSAR. What a star! And her confidence had shot not only through the roof, but out through the door, and this became part of her charming personality.

Over the year Bill and I attended many of her fundraising events, always buying our own tickets to assist with the charity affair. Many of these occasions were held at Ferneham

Hall as it could cater for hundreds of guests. There were many engagements organised to raise money for these three charities and it was a very packed calendar. The Last Night of the Proms and a Glenn Miller concert were just two of the highlights, finishing with the Mayor's Charity Ball. This began with a splendid dinner, the music provided by the Royal Marines Dance Band performing toe-tapping melodies in their spectacular evening dress. Susan raised £6,000 for TRADISSAR. What an amazing effort, and no doubt the other charities were just as grateful!

CHAPTER TWENTY-EIGHT

Alfi and Magnus's Story

As promised, Waveney organised another para-training day to be held at Crofton. We were jubilant and once more there were many riders hoping to fill the day's programme. She had asked Clive to be the coach on this occasion. She would judge the riders' tests and Clive would then help them to improve on their performance and scores. I'd given specific slot times to my riders so Waveney and Clive had their work cut out during a very full day.

We were well into the day when Debbie, who was now the owner of Alfi, burst into the school leading an enormous horse whose ribs and backbone were unmistakeable. "Look what I've just found!"

All the riding came to a halt to inspect this new arrival.

My brain began working overtime. Side-saddle was flashing into my mind and luckily I had two in my car. I had one brought in without any hesitation and I heaved it up on to this gentle giant's back myself. It was a surprisingly good fit and everyone was stunned.

"I want you to have him," said Debbie.

Clive's reaction was "Only Rayna would put a side-saddle on a carthorse!"

Debbie and her husband, Graham Froome, were now the owners of two big horses and they insisted that they should be RDA horses. This was a kind and generous offer, especially as Debbie had chosen to house them at another yard about a mile away. So, each Monday she would religiously transport her two boys to Crofton for our use.

Magnus began to fill out and put on weight and muscle. He was soon looking very handsome, with feathered feet the size of buckets and a long mane and tail. He had taken to side-saddle like a duck to water and he was a lot of fun for me to ride. I was hoping to make him more like a dressage horse than a carthorse.

We had a new rider, Shelley Rees, who had joined us recently, and she very much wanted to do side-saddle. She bravely accepted Magnus to be her mount. Then we got news that Fern's owner couldn't keep her any longer. Tia was very sad as she had been riding her for some years. Tia was progressing marvellously at this point, and we tried desperately hard to find her a replacement from the selection of ponies already at Crofton. Then one day Clair Lucas, Tia's mum, told us that she'd seen a lovely pony that she thought they might be able to purchase. Barren soon arrived at the school and a new chapter began for Tia. Clair was a hard-working, animal-loving single mum who was prepared to do anything to keep Tia riding.

It so happened that Selina and Daisy could do with more help looking after Lucky. I suggested this to Clair and she was happy to become a groom, giving Selina some relief. This arrangement worked well for several years.

We needed Cindy, our president, to come and check our progress with our new acquisitions. She agreed that given the right training and care Magnus and Barren might very well be suitable for the new role that they were being slotted into.

Several students were now riding Magnus regularly, and I enjoyed riding him myself when he wasn't required for training purposes.

Debbie suggested that I enter him in an unaffiliated dressage competition. She turned him out beautifully, whitening

Deborah Miller passes her grade test.

Maeve, hacking out in fields, with Yeoman.

Training day at Broadlands RDA Centre.

*Kevin Reeves receiving grade III in riding and horse care
from Trish Willetts.*

TRADISSAR riders waiting their turn.

*Kevin and Sarah giving a display on Lucky in fancy dress for charity –
£150 was collected.*

Kevin cleaning out the stables.

Kevin.

Kevin and Lucky.

Photo courtesy of Derry Moore
President of the Association Mrs Betty Skelton (mounted, left) with her
daughter Jinks Bryer (standing, far right), granddaughters Cindy Sims
(standing, left) Pippa Stacy (centre) and great granddaughter Olivia Sims
(mounted, right) This photo first appeared in Country Life March 2, 2000.

Caroline filling a hay net, part of the Education Programme.

Some members of the first TRADISSAR Committee team.

Anthony Head, TRADISSAR's patron.

Meeting Lee Pearson for the first time.

The Mayor of Fareham.

*Tia being coached by Simon Lauren, para-coach, with Waveney Luke,
the RDA's dressage selector.*

Michael Lane on Matilda.

Simon and Rayna coaching Jo, who lost weight so she could ride.

Christmas at 1600.

*Side-saddle display on large horses at Baughurst RDA
fortieth-anniversary celebration.*

Three lovely big bums!

Piggyback to the party!

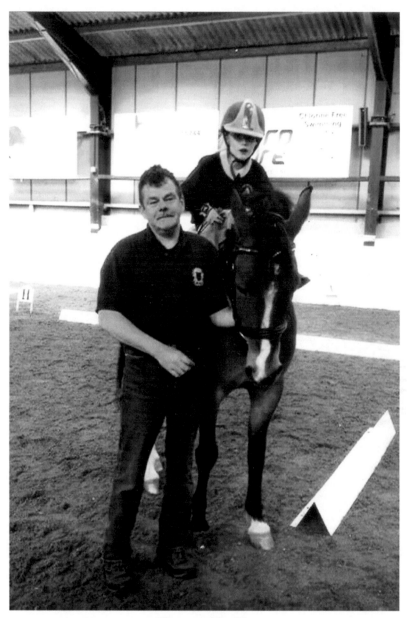

Clive coaching Tia.

Anne Coney (right), Shelley Milburn (left), and Tia.

Diane Pettet on Lucky at the RDA nationals, Hartpury.

191

PR for TRADISSAR at Countrywide, 2011–12.

Charlie Dimmock and Rayna with Charles Duf on his
cycle ride for charity.

his wonderful feathered feet and plaiting his mane and tail in the traditional Clydesdale way. He seemed to work well in the warm-up, and didn't seem to mind having so many other horses around, and he was also fine when we were in the indoor school. However, when he entered the outdoor dressage arena he appeared somewhat overwhelmed by all the bunting and distractions. He was certainly eye-catching, and the judge, I assume, wondered how he would perform. I did my best to keep us both together, but, although he was fairly obedient, there was clearly much work to be done to improve his balance and confidence.

Debbie was thrilled with his act and conduct and we received a score of 59% for a 'walk and trot' test. Debbie was keen to take 'her boys' to South Bucks for training days, and Shelley, who was riding Magnus regularly, and Jo, who had a super partnership with Alfi, were thrilled to go. Tia was now getting more confident with Barren and they were in regular attendance at South Bucks.

Meanwhile, Di and Jo had been doing some serious preparation for the RDA nationals. Lucky, despite her twenty-three years, was still functioning at a high level, but it would be a big new event for Alfi. The transporter arrived and horses, gear, feed and Matilda were loaded on board. It was a three-hour journey to Hartpury College, and we made quite a convoy. As we came into the vicinity of Hartpury, Di told us later, Lucky let out a loud whinny. Could this be a good omen for Di? Lucky was now on familiar territory and seemed to know it. The two horses had travelled well and were now happily stabled next to each other. In the cool of the evening, Di and I decided to take them out for a hack around the college fields – they loved it! Lucky was full of anticipation for the next day and was in high spirits, while Alfi was just taking everything in his stride.

Jane, my friend and long-time groom, joined us and Lucy accompanied us as a groom for Jo. Both horses and riders were immaculately turned out. Di was first to enter the arena – quite a daunting experience for a first-timer – but the partnership between horse and rider worked well under the eager eyes of the gallery. We left Jo after she'd had a warm-up as we wanted to get good seats to watch her performance. As we sat in the arena where we were expecting to see Jo do her test a string of riders came and went, but still no Jo. The class appeared to be over, and everyone was packing up their things, when Jo and Alfi entered. What had happened? Jane and I went around to the office to enquire. For some strange reason she had not been called into the ring when it was her time to enter, and Jo, being unsure herself of the importance of watching one's time and keeping in touch with the stewards, had missed her slot. The judge had, so she thought, finished a big class and was ready to pack up. She was a bit cross at having another late rider turn up, but let her take her test anyway. Unfortunately, her mount was also in a bad mood by this point and performed rather poorly. Poor Jo – what a bitter lesson she'd learnt! Then, to balance this sad story, she was presented with her Carl Hester reins and a gold medal for winning her class in Dressage Anywhere, all in full view of a cheering audience, and that was a serious success story.

Not long after the RDA nationals, Cindy arranged to have a little show at Holloway House, her home. It was mostly a side-saddle show, so Lucky, Magnus and Barren were all invited, along with as many riders as we could rustle up to show off their skills. Cindy had big fields to warm up in and a little indoor school, but her large outdoor manége was where all the performances were done. The seats were arranged so that every member of the audience had a super view of the arena. Our members were competing against able-bodied riders, many of them Cindy's own students, and this was nerve-racking at times. Strict instructions were given not to go out of one's comfort zone at any time. Walk, and a short trot if feeling confident, but not canter. Magnificent Magnus gained himself a fan club. Barren behaved well enough once Cindy had thoroughly knocked all the beans out of him on the end of a lunge rein. Poor Lucky, despite trying to be her usual professional self, struggled with a surface which had become well worked over by the other horses. Her age was beginning to show and she needed a lot of care and attention from her rider to keep her happy now. It was a really fun day and so lovely to be out of doors and in the sunshine. To round off the day's adventure there was a class of ladies in historical costumes – a concours d'élégance is always a crowd-pleaser, and a spectacle that our TRADISSAR members were seeing for the first time.

CHAPTER TWENTY-NINE

Baughurst RDA Anniversary

The Baughurst RDA group was to celebrate their fortieth anniversary in the autumn of 2013. I was contacted by the group organiser, Brenda Woods, who invited TRADISSAR not only to share in their special day, but also to provide the entertainment for the occasion. The invitation was a great honour and we wanted to make it a first-class display of TRADISSAR's skills and accomplishments.

I'd been invited to take part in a number of anniversaries – one that stands out was at Wormwood Scrubs. Sister Mary Joy was friends with royalty, and Princess Anne opened her school. I was part of the day's entertainment, along with the Metropolitan mounted police force.

With three lovable big horses ready for our use, and lots of other talent besides, we began to put a challenging programme together. We hoped the weather would be kind to us on the day as we were set to perform in a large field in the presence of around 200 guests. The day was soon upon us, a Sunday, and, as often happens with the best-laid plans, things began to go horribly wrong. The first blow came when the transporter let us down; we needed to get three large horses and a pony to a venue which was almost two hours' drive away.

I can state with confidence that many times in the past the TRADISSARs had risen to the occasion and found ways around our difficulties. We put our heads together and the mobile phones went into action. One of our new members had just recently bought a lorry which was suitable to take all the horses; however, Kelly, the owner, didn't have a licence to drive it. Clair had a cheeky thought – to give her old boyfriend a call and see if he could give up his Sunday for the good of TRADISSAR. Yes! Steve was free, had his licence and would be there shortly. A great cheer went up. Once Steve arrived, the horses were quickly loaded on board and we set off in convoy for the village of Baughurst, also in Hampshire. We arrived at the beautiful venue with just minutes to spare and were met by a much relieved Brenda. She had the pony which their group used ready for us to meet. He was a chunky little chap, and Tia was going to give a little display on him under Jo's instruction. She was also going to give a side-saddle show on Diva, the pony she was riding at the time.

Our friend Philippa had offered to loan us another big bay horse so we could form a quadrille. We needed to get Lucky and the other two boys ready quickly, but we were biting our nails down in the hope that Philippa would turn up soon. Time was ticking away and we couldn't wait any longer for our fourth member to join us. It turned out that Philippa was still by the roadside, with a most disgruntled horse who was becoming angrier by the minute, waiting for help to change a flat tyre.

All our helpers were well rehearsed and under my and Jo's supervision. On command, they went into action – fitting side-saddles on Lucky and Magnus, Alfi's cross-saddle and all the sparkling bridles and bits. We disabled riders had to be mounted with only the bare minimum of facilities – just what was kept in a barn and an enormous field.

All three of us were mounted on our beautifully turned-out horses with a minimum of fuss, and we made our entry before an enthusiastic audience. Introductions were made and we could tell that our entrance had had quite an impact. Nothing had been rehearsed – due to space restrictions at Crofton – nor had we performed in such a large field before, never mind to such a distinguished audience. I trusted our horses and I knew that our riders would give their best for the occasion. My riders were pretty experienced at riding for visitors and examiners alike. They had also competed and trained outside their TRADISSAR familiarity and loved to show off what they had learnt.

Unfortunately, we were not able to set up any music to ride to, but this didn't put the horses off exploring their new space. They were keen to use every inch of the field's surface, making it possible to do large circles and serpentines. We began by playing follow the leader and then gradually built on top of that, with riders and horses coming together to show our excellent control skills in formation. Hopefully, we had demonstrated what TRADISSAR could do.

The performance ended with a great ovation and then the horses needed to be packed off home with their grooms so that the members of TRADISSAR could join the party.

A wonderful marquee had been erected on the lawn for the festivities. The closest thing to transport I could find to get from my car to the marquee was by piggyback, as the wheelchair would not have given a good ride over the manicured lawn.

We were served a banquet of goodies to eat and drink. We were also treated to a slice from an enormous cake which had been made in the shape of a horse's head, decorated in icing, and with a big 'forty' in the middle.

We had been invited to share in this special occasion with a well-established and respected group who had a history and track record going back for forty years – a remarkable achievement for TRADISSAR.

CHAPTER THIRTY

Last Run In

Our first event in 2014 was Dressage Anywhere, and five of our riders were already making preparations to compete. Jo, who had been so successful on Alfi, was grounded. While dismounting one day, she miscalculated the distance between herself and the ground. Her helpers were there doing their job, but somehow she had lost her balance and slipped through their fingers, falling to the ground and hurting her good leg. When the day came, instead of performing in Dressage Anywhere, she had to content herself with being the cameraman. A new rider, Sophie, was given the honour of riding Alfi.

Lucky was still able to function well enough for Di to compete at the high level she was aiming for, but this did require some additional medical care. Shelley wanted to have a go on Magnus – side-saddle, of course! Vanessa was in good form on her own horse, Kiwi, and Tia wanted to introduce Barren to professional RDA riding. It was going to be an interesting class.

Debbie, who had competed on her own horse, Memphis, was unavailable this time round, but her daughter Lucy had been proving herself an excellent helper. She was a capable rider and could manage all the horses with notable skill and experience. We paired her up with Tia and Barren and found that she had a clever way to keep him under control, while still letting Tia skilfully ride him through the tests. This would make an excellent combination for our entry into the RDA regionals at South Bucks in a few weeks' time.

Riders and horses looked the part as they rode through their tests, usually improving each time they did it. Jo and I resumed our roles as video editors before sending them off for judging.

It was soon Easter and Di had been hard at work preparing to do her Bronze Certificate. She spent many hours with Cindy to ensure both her knowledge and riding skills were at their peak for this exam. We were delighted to learn that Jilly Roper would be the examiner, as she'd visited us previously and we all got on very well. Unfortunately, when it came to the day of the test Lucky was not happy enough to do the job. Di had to pick a new horse right at the last minute, and Alfi was chosen as a suitable stand-in. Although Jilly is a very thorough examiner, and in spite of the eleventh-hour horse swap, Di came through with flying colours. We were eager for Jilly to see our Magnus in action. She was very approving and said that her group had also used draught horses successfully.

We were also proud to host a visitor from New Zealand, Angela Hutchinson, who was visiting the UK on a fact-finding mission for her own RDA group. She spent the day with us at Crofton and was fascinated by our big horses and side-saddle riders. She would have some interesting stories to take home to her group.

To get me on some of these big horses was quite a skill. Most mounting blocks have steps to get the rider up to a suitable height, but I can't do steps without the help of two or three helpers. All I really need is a leg up, and most horsey people understand that – they just have to guide my right leg where it needs to be. I can take it from there. Of course, things could occasionally go a bit wrong. Once, as I went up, my leg was thrown over the horse's back; I ended up sitting on the horse's bum, having completely missed the saddle. Such mishaps were usually a source of great amusement. However, lifting me up from the horse's rear and getting me into the side-saddle, which rode about six inches above the animal's back, or a cross-saddle if it had a high cantle, was quite a lot more difficult than getting me up there from a grounded start. Then there was always that one assistant who had more muscle and energy than was really required to lift up my seven-stone body. The result of this would be that I nearly ended up over the other side and someone would have to react quickly to rescue me.

CHAPTER THIRTY-ONE

Regional Preparation

May was approaching swiftly, and once again our riders were preparing for their entries at the South Bucks regionals. I asked Di Redfern if she could spare Clive for a day to give my riders and horses some last-minute coaching. She was happy to loan him to us, and Clive was glad to offer his services once more. Several of our good riders were out of action this year, as often happens when disabled people try to function at their maximum level for too long.

Only four riders were available on the day, but I thought this could also be a good opportunity for me to showcase Alfi and Magnus and get some feedback from Clive. Both these horses needed to be exercised correctly to keep them going at their best for their not-so-experienced riders.

Clive was very popular with our riders. It was said "that he coached more para-rider silver and gold medallists than anyone else in the world", and it was true! Shelley and Tia had both been to training days at South Bucks, and more recently young Sophie had been joining them. She was a teenager who had had surgery to remove cancer from her right leg, but at this time she was in excellent physical shape.

Like many girls of her age she could be a bit unruly at times, and we had to withdraw her riding rights as a punishment at least once. Nevertheless, Debbie found a useful helper in Sophie and let her ride Alfi around her yard during the week. This young lady had bags of energy and enthusiasm which needed careful handling to keep horse and rider safe. However, in Clive she had found someone to idolise, and it looked as though he rather enjoyed the challenge of a keen young rider.

Things had not gone so well for Tia. Lucy, her specialist helper, had sadly met with a terrible accident while riding her motorbike the week before and was still in hospital. In Dressage Anywhere she led Tia's pony, Barren, with a canny skill, teaching Tia to ride her test with the confidence to gain good scores and remarks. I was in a dilemma. I couldn't think of a suitable replacement to step into Lucy's shoes for the regional championships, and I didn't want to disappoint young Tia.

I had hopes that Clive might know of a South Bucks helper who could become Tia's surrogate, guiding her through the warm-up stage on the day, which would have to be done in a field. Tia would be fine during the actual test as she was now able to ride her pony independently. If this was not going to be possible then Barren would have to be lunged beforehand, or I would ride him during the warm-up to make sure that he lost any over-exuberant attitude before his young rider took over the reins.

Clive's solution was to invite Tia and Barren to South Bucks for the weekend. This would give them both time to settle into their new surroundings, and they would also benefit from another coaching session. The day of the regionals, which was a Sunday, was a very early morning start for all our riders, helpers and horses, but all arrived in good time at the South Bucks venue. Debbie, her husband, Graham, and young Sophie travelled with Alfi and Magnus. Di and Sophie were to ride Alfi, and Shelley was looking forward to competing on Magnus. Di had an early time for her test, so she hastily warmed up Alfi and we saw her safely into the arena to watch her performance. When we returned to our base camp, Debbie, Magnus, and Sophie weren't anywhere to be seen. I remembered that Clive had instructed Debbie to warm up Magnus herself. At the time I wondered about the wisdom of that plan, but Debbie was set on it.

The next thing I knew was that there had been an accident involving Magnus. Sophie had ridden into a tree branch, had badly hurt her nose, and now an ambulance had been called for. What a terrible shock! But of more immediate concern was what had Sophie been doing riding Magnus anyway? I thought that they were under Clive's supervision, so how could this happen? My head was in a spin and this was turning out to be an annus horribilis for TRADISSAR. The next measures taken were even more serious – Magnus was labelled a 'dangerous horse' and was not to be ridden.

I felt this was a very unfair sentence to subject him to. There is a saying, 'It's not the horse at fault; look at the rider.' Poor Shelley didn't have a mount now, and Sophie was taken off to hospital and scratched from the competition.

Shelley, not to be beaten, said that she would like to do her test on Alfi, riding cross-saddle. This was a serious challenge for her as she had never ridden Alfi before and had some reservations about cross-saddle. She entered the arena and I called her test for her. Blow me down! She won the class with a score in the high 60s, which qualified her to compete in the nationals.

For some reason, Tia, under Clive's supervision, was now riding her test cross-saddle. I suspect that a professional person I know had deliberately warned Tia and her mother, Claire, that riding side-saddle would 'twist her hips'. They were devastated and confused by this overpowering statement – this was a total misconception of side-saddle riding and, of course, totally untrue. Besides, she had been doing it for nearly four years without any problems and it had been of enormous benefit to her. Unfortunately there are some hidebound people who think they're always right and who can convince others of their convictions. She was beaten by just one mark to come in second.

The day was full of mixed blessings, but the outcome was rather sad. It heralded the beginning of the end for TRADISSAR RDA. That was the last regional championship to be held at South Bucks, after some twenty or more years of success for many riders.

Sophie was not seriously hurt and her mother was quite dismissive of her experience. Alfi and Magnus moved to Cornwall a year or so later, and Tia and Barren also moved away. Shelly is still riding strongly and is a frequent visitor to South Bucks, where Di Redfern and I continue to be her mentors.

CHAPTER THIRTY-TWO

Lucky's Swansong

Lucky had missed all the excitement leading up to the day of the regional championships due to medical concerns. She had been showing signs of stiffness and tensions in her right hind leg, more noticeable at the canter. Murray, our super vet, had given her a whole battery of treatments, which in the past had been very successful, but this time around she didn't seem to be improving. We had accompanied the vet's treatments with appropriate physio and exercise, along with a period of rest. Lucky's mind was still as sharp as ever, but it seemed to me that her physical frame wasn't as supple as it should be and she just wasn't bouncing back after her expert care.

In desperation, and as a special favour, I asked my friends Steve and Stormy if they would come and look at Lucky. They were in the alternative medical practice and had kept me pain-free and able to function at my most able for a number of years. Reluctantly, they came to see Lucky. I was fascinated to watch them transferring human practice to an animal. They had enormous sympathy and insight into how Lucky was feeling and responding to them.

Then it became difficult for Lucky to pick up her hind leg for me to clean her hooves, and each day I was becoming more dependent on Selina and Claire's help. Gradually she became more and more distressed at being asked to pick up her foot, and she was totally unable to hold it up when the blacksmith came to shoe her, even under the mild sedative which had been recommended by Murray. Lucky was an animal that wanted to please at all costs, so we knew that we were dealing with a serious problem. At this stage it wasn't too great a concern and, as she wasn't currently being ridden by anyone, she could happily go without hind shoes for the time being.

Selina had experience of laminitis in her pony, and didn't want the worry of that again, so she made sure to carefully monitor Lucky's diet. Lucky was still going out into the field every day to see her friends and seemed to be enjoying life.

Each day I would be sure to visit Lucky in her stable, giving her lots of love and attention, and we would talk together to pass the time away. One particular day, before I even had time to park my car, which was right next to Lucky's stable, both Claire and Selina were there to meet me. I could tell immediately that all was not well, and Lucky hadn't shown herself at the stable door to welcome me. My heart began to sink a little, but I had to ask the question "Is everything all right?"

Claire began by explaining that she had taken Lucky down to see her friends in the field. She'd been reluctant to go, but went after a little persuasion. Instead of trotting off to join her friends, she made it clear that she didn't want to stay, so Claire had taken it upon herself to bring her straight home. Claire called Selina, who was quite upset to see that Lucky was quite lame. She now seemed to be in a lot of pain, despite the medication she was on.

Lucky was usually bright-eyed, looking out for my arrival, and I had always got a whinny and a "Welcome, Mum!" but not today. The three of us put our heads and hearts together. They wanted to protect me from any pain, but I could read their minds.

"Is this serious?" I began.

"Yes!" they said, hesitantly, dropping their gaze from mine.

"Do you think that Lucky has had enough? Should we call Malcolm, our local vet?"

Again, it was a "Yes!"

We knew that we'd done everything possible to ensure Lucky was kept happy, content and able to function at her best. For the past couple of months Lucky's health had been deteriorating and she hadn't responded well to her usual treatments. She really seemed to have given up the fight.

Malcolm arrived and he read our thoughts, saving us any further interpretation of events and the present situation. We took Lucky out behind the stables, to a quiet, grassy place, away from prying eyes, and there she went down, her dignity intact, and with us all present to say a final farewell. The life just went out of her the moment she hit the ground. All three of us – Selina, Clair and I – burst into floods of tears. It was so sad to see this beautiful, noble creature that we all knew so well, suddenly expressionless. Eventually we pulled ourselves together. We all felt a strange sense of guilt at not being strong enough to cope, let alone be stoic enough to console each other with this terrible moment of grief and loss. Malcolm returned after tactfully giving us some time alone with Lucky. We were embarrassed that he should find us in this tearful state and apologised for it.

"I'd have been worried if you hadn't responded this way" was his comforting answer.

So it was that Lucky passed away with grace, as she deserved, surrounded by those who loved her.

A few days later I received a kind note from Malcolm reassuring me there wasn't any doubt that we'd done everything in our power to give Lucky a happy and fulfilling life – such a nice gesture. I went home to Bill and, with a lump in my throat, told him the sad news.

His response was, as always, understanding and uplifting. "Let's go out and buy a tree to commemorate Lucky's life" was Bill's suggestion.

So, in Lucky's name, we planted a beautiful pink camellia

bush in our garden, and it is still blooming to this day.

Lucky had been the most intelligent and companionable horse I'd ever owned. She hadn't reached the heights of schooling and top tiers of competing that I'd hoped for, though she had the brain for it. Her fitness levels seemed marred by some small injury which didn't show up on an X-ray. Although she had a magnificent trot, and was able to collect up to show some piaffe and passage steps, she found it difficult to develop flying changes. In the end I felt it would be cruel to push her any further and that the strict training regimen we worked to needed to be relaxed. However, she made the perfect schoolmistress for my disabled riders. Many of them learnt to ride side-saddle on Lucky, and she was still a perfect mount for use at the RDA competitions. Several of my riders won their Bronze Certificates while riding on Lucky, and I often rode her when teaching, to demonstrate certain skills.

She knew the difference between a child rider and a more experienced one, and was trustworthy at all times. Despite my physical vulnerability, I was able to hack out with her knowing that she would be sensible in any emergency. One of our favourite places to venture together was the Titchfield Haven National Nature Reserve, down the coast at Hill Head. One day, walking along the road, with the marshlands to our left and the seafront on our right, we came across a large swan on the verges of the marsh. Was he going to cross the road, or perhaps was he lost?. Lucky had seen him too, but kept on going. I knew Lucky's temperament very well by now, and I'd learnt to allay any doubts I might have and trust her better judgement. As we approached the swan, he flew at her, hissing and flapping his wings in a very frightening manner. I was most unnerved; I was riding cross-saddle, for this was road walking, and I was not as secure in my seat as I would have been had I been side-saddle. As this bird came at Lucky we were both terribly startled, me more than her, but she bravely stood her ground. Fortunately a passer-by intervened and saw the creature off. It seemed that the poor bird was only protecting his wife and family, but it had given me quite a shake-up nonetheless. Lucky continued on her way, seemingly undisturbed by the incident. I was very grateful to her for keeping such a level head. Lucky had proven herself the ultimate trustworthy companion once again, and it had been an honour and privilege to share nine years of our lives together.

CHAPTER THIRTY-THREE

Full Circle

It's been two years since Lucky passed away. Our lives are just as busy and we still remain deeply involved with assisting others to follow their equestrian dreams and aspirations. Bill complains each day that he never has enough time to sit down and work on his model aircraft or read his fantasy fiction, but I know he loves the life we've chosen to live together.

After such an eventful few decades I decided it was time to sit down and write my story. Very fortunately, I had kept detailed diaries that went back twenty-five years. It was Clive who, in a 'wisdom of Solomon' moment, told me that I should start keeping a diary of my training days when I was at South Bucks. This I did religiously, not because I had any plans at the time but because I felt a need to record the events of those developing years.

With the passing of Lucky I had no way to keep fit and missed very much the companionship that comes with riding your own horse. Some of my riders from TRADISSAR also missed her dearly as she'd been the pillar to which the whole school was anchored. Returning to South Bucks, I explained our situation in a long conversation with Di Redfern, the owner. She was very quick to invite us to ride her horses, all in a safe and secure environment. This has been almost like a homecoming, returning once more to where my story began.

Clive, who was as much a part of South Bucks as Di and the

horses that lived there, had moved on. He is now a freelance international para-coach and a 'man of the world'. Just recently, as fate would have it, he returned to England and was invited back to South Bucks to fill in the gap left by Helen, the present instructor, who was unavailable that day. I also happened to be there that day, with Shelley, to ride. Shelley was mounted on her favourite horse, Mable, a pretty dark-bay mare with a soft temperament, and I was given an old schoolmaster named Yogi. Then who should enter the school but dear old Clive and Di! It felt just like old times! Di sat back to observe the whole show and Clive stood in the middle of the arena and asked the familiar question "What are you wanting to achieve in this session?" Shelley knew of Clive's achievements and was quite the devotee; she couldn't believe her luck. I was also very happy to get any input from Clive as to how my horse was going. My role at South Bucks is to keep the dear old schoolmaster horses happy and functioning at their best. This saves their instructors time. Both Shelley and I had a most enjoyable session, and Clive and I exchanged a great deal of reminiscent banter.

This was early in 2016, and the para-riders were preparing to go to Rio for that year's Paralympic Games. South Bucks is still a centre of excellence for such riders to train, so the place buzzed with reporters and photographers from the media, all hoping to scoop a story before the talented team headed off to Brazil. Di had bought herself a beautiful mare by the name of Athena, for Sophie Christiansen to compete on, and this beautiful creature was quite the favourite with the press.

I've also taken the time to become a listed British Dressage judge. Though I've spent over ten years judging unaffiliated dressage, it is quite an achievement to be able to judge the more advanced classes. I'm always keen to attend the BD judge-training days and conferences. These always help one to work towards maintaining the very high standards and principles of the sport.

I'm still in touch with my two grooms, Jane and Wendy, and also my friend Rebekah, who were all part of my team in those competing years. Jane went on to do a wonderful job as groom for a lady named Deborah Collins, who owned and trained horses to Grand Prix level. She eventually had to leave her job, however, as she and her partner Paul had a baby boy, Benjamin, who is now about six months old. Wendy went to live on the North Island of New Zealand. She and Bruce work their extensive livestock farm together, where they make good use of Bruce's latest acquisition – an aeroplane! Just recently she was home in England visiting her family. We spent a very happy day together, along with her parents, Cliffe and Geraldene. Sadly, Wendy's parents and Bill now share an unfortunate problem – both have been diagnosed with early stage Alzheimer's.

Rebekah, along with her horse, Azbo, continues to attend as many SSA events as she can and still competes at the nationals. She is a busy lady, working full time as an occupational therapist, and must juggle work, quality time with her loving husband, Andrew, and the care and maintenance of Azbo.

Some of my precious gear and saddles have been passed on to people just starting out in the world of competitive side-saddle. One of my smaller side-saddles has gone to a disabled little girl. The mother was thrilled that the side-saddle fitted the pony and that her little daughter would be able to ride more safely this way.

My historical costumes have got an airing from time to time at lectures or displays, where I give tips and advice to newcomers who want to compete in these elegant classes.

I recently enjoyed catching up with old friends at the SSA nationals show at Addington. It's so interesting to see how the sport is changing, with a new generation of ladies pursuing their dreams and ambitions just as I did many years ago. In November this year we got to see the magnificent Lippizaner horses, from the Spanish Riding School in Vienna, riding their quadrilles to Viennese music and performing *la science et l'art de l'équitation*. There is still a wonderful world of horses out there!

And so life goes on. I hope that I'll always be connected with horses and those who look after them, and that I'll still be able to offer the odd suggestion towards their success, even though I may no longer be able to ride – though that's still far off, God willing. For me, horses and riding are the be-all and end-all of life's enjoyment. Long may I continue to take pleasure from these activities!